# WINNING THE TRANSITION GAME

## Lessons from the Trenches

# WINNNG THE TRANSITION GAME:

## Lessons from the Trenches

Adonal Foyle, MBA, MA

Copyright © 2020 Adonal Foyle Enterprises

All rights reserved. No part of this book may be reproduced, stored, or transmitted by any means whether auditory, graphic, mechanical, or electronic without written permission of both publisher and author, except in the case of brief excerpts used in critical articles and reviews. Unauthorized reproduction of any part of this work is illegal and is punishable by law.

Second Edition

ISBN-13: 978-1-944662-58-5
Previous ISBN-13: 978-1-944662-49-3

Realization Press

Publishing date: 1/2/2021

Cover Design and illustrations by MASgraphicarts.com

# Dedication

To basketball Hall of Famer and my friend, Nate Thurmond:

Our friend has gone to sleep, but the quilt of excellence that hangs in our collective memory will forever be the template of his immortality.

To Roy Byrd Sr.
For a life of service to our country and our community.
This book is for you and the legacy you left behind.

# Table of Contents

Dedication ................................................................................................. v

Foreword ................................................................................................. xi

Introduction Journey into Discovery ................................................. xv

**Part I: REALITY**

Chapter One The Faces of Transition ................................................. 3

Chapter Two Phase 1: Ambivalence ................................................. 13

Chapter Three Phase 2: Searching ..................................................... 29

Chapter Four Phase 3: Anxiety .......................................................... 37

**Part II: CROSSOVER**

Chapter Five Phase 4: The Epiphany ................................................ 49

Chapter Six Shifting your Mindset: Reclaiming the Word "Retire" ....... 59

Chapter Seven Finding your Purpose Again .................................... 65

**Part III: WINNING THE TRANSITION GAME**

Chapter Eight 20 Ways to Win The Transition Game .................... 77

Chapter Nine Transition Stories from the Trenches ....................... 93

Conclusion Rediscovering Your Inner Athlete ............................... 175

| | |
|---|---|
| Acknowledgements | 181 |
| Resources | 184 |
| About the Author | 187 |
| Other Books from Adonal Foyle | 190 |
| Ordering Information | 194 |
| References | 195 |

# Praise for Winning the Transition Game

"I am still trying to figure out my transition. I am currently playing in the Big3 league. Transition is not only about finding that next career... it's about finding peace within yourself and knowing that your life isn't over just because your playing career is."

**Jason Richardson**
**Former NBA player**

"I had the opportunity to have Adonal as a teammate toward the end of my career. And even though he was still at his prime, he was already thinking about what the next phase of his life would look like. Winning the Transition Game is the result of years of research, interviews and first-hand experience that can't be underestimated. Having gone through different careers after my playing days, I know I could have benefitted from a tool like this during my own transition."

**Chris Mullin**
**Basketball Hall-of-Famer**
**Olympic Gold Medalist**

"Winning the Transition Game is about taking ownership of your transition process from professional sports. But it's more than that... It's about how we approach the second stage of our lives. As a former WNBA player, I understand this process more than most, and Adonal's book offers tools that will help a lot of athletes better transition from their sport, and toward the next chapter."

**Ruthie Bolton**
**Former WNBA player**
**Two-time Olympic Gold Medalist**

*Adonal Foyle, MA, MBA*

"In the short time I've gotten to know Adonal, I learned that he genuinely wants to help people. Whether it's children through his foundation, or professional athletes through this book. Winning the Transition Game could have been useful when I retired from football in 2009. Now, players past and present have a tool on how to adjust when it comes to finding that post-playing career."

**Jeremy Newberry**
**Former NFL player**

"Adonal has been a friend and mentor since my first day in the league. Having played with him for two franchises, I saw him constantly working on his finances while traveling on the plane. Since that day, I always asked him questions - from finances to a post-playing career. He was always happy to share his knowledge with me. Now, with Winning the Transition Game, he is sharing that knowledge with everyone."

**Mickaël Piétrus**
**Former NBA Player**
**International Basketball Star**

"Adonal was a great teammate and an even better friend. I was happy to share my insights on what transitioning out of basketball meant to me, and now I'm glad he's sharing these perspectives with other players. Winning the Transition Game is a long overdue tool that will prove to be useful to current and former players."

**Antawn Jamison**
**Former NBA Player**

# Foreword

## By Bob Delaney, Retired NBA Referee

The American experience is one of transition and constant change. Our society started with a town crier sharing news in a town center and we now live drinking from a fire hose of information. I am writing this foreword 35,000 feet in the air traveling from New York City to San Francisco. We have the expectation that everything we need is at our fingertips at all times. The guy seated next to me is upset because the airline Wi-Fi is intermittent! I blame McDonald's because once we got hamburgers on demand... we wanted everything in life the same way: with all deliberate speed.

I believe that a successful transition can be achieved by using the following formula:

*Experience + Intellectual Readiness + Reflection = Effective Development and Growth*

We all have *Experiences,* and, if we share our experiences, we learn from each other. Experiential learning is a major part of our foundation and many times the learning comes with a test before we even know the material. Experience can be the result of hard knocks. Our experiences become an important element when contemplating our retirement strategies. We must become mindful of our experiences and use them as the basis to help rebuild our retirement future.

*Adonal Foyle, MA, MBA*

Secondly, our **Intellectual Readiness** is an important way to increase our retirement success. Intellectual readiness can be formal education or informal learning. Formal learning is the studying of subjects through education that graduates to specific training for a profession. For example, at 56 years of age I went back to school at St. Mary's College of California for a Leadership Master's Degree. I wanted to learn about leadership from the academic community.

Intellectual readiness from an informal perspective involves learning outside of a formal educational structure like your home and work place. My life's journey presented numerous opportunities for informal learning. I learned about leadership across the dining room table with my parents being the first leaders in my life. I was truly raised by a village with my grandparents, aunts, uncles, teachers, coaches, and neighbors having an influence in my life. I experienced leadership playing basketball and baseball in high school and college. I observed leadership when I was a New Jersey State Trooper and when I worked undercover infiltrating the Mafia in the 1970s—you can learn from negative as well as positive. I saw leadership during my NBA referee career and as NBA Vice President of Referee Operations and Director of Officials. I saw leadership daily as the Southeastern Conference Special Advisor for Officiating Development/Performance. Intellectual readiness therefore is another important element that can be a significant factor necessary to fully achieve our retirement goal of a successful transition.

The last part of the formula is the most difficult because **Reflection** is not always part of our process. Reflection means thinking deeply about your experiences. Let's say you are at work and you have your feet up on your desk, hands locked behind your head, looking out the window and your "boss" walks by and asks "What are you doing?" and your response is "Oh, I am reflecting, ma'am." How do you think that will be received? We are doers and reflection is not an encouraged behavior. But it is very important for us to reflect on what is happening. Especially during transitions, reflection is important because all transitions are difficult. In summary, our own individual Experiences combined with intellectual Readiness and Reflections can lead to effective development and growth. Put another way, this formula can serve as the foundational elements necessary to achieve a successful transition.

I personally have been through many transitions in my professional life. My NBA career began in 1985 with the referee development program (Continental Basketball Association—CBA) and I was hired full-time in 1987. I ran the NBA floors until 2011 and took one year away from basketball before transitioning to NBA Referee Operations management where I served as Crew Chief Development Advisor and then as Vice President Director of Officials.

Many of the transition emotions and feelings Adonal addresses in this book came back to me as I was reading. I continue to navigate some of those emotions to this day. Transitions take time. Recently, a friend and I were on an island beach enjoying a vacation with our wives when we had a conversation about how "strange and guilty" we felt not working full-time. We are both consulting and staying busy, yet the rhythm of full-time work was no longer part of our daily routine. How we navigate those emotions is what matters. Sharing our feelings with someone who has or is experiencing a similar emotion validates our thoughts and gives us permission to have honest discussions. Peer-to-peer. Our conversations on the beach that day helped us both understand more fully the transition journey we shared.

We all have multiple transitions during our lives. In 1789 Benjamin Franklin famously stated, "In this world nothing can be said to be certain, except death and taxes." Adonal Foyle clearly defines the certainty of transitions and you are about to gain a competitive edge in... Winning the Transition Game.

*Adonal Foyle, MA, MBA*

My life has been a kaleidoscope of experiences including being a New Jersey State Trooper, an NBA Referee, NBA Vice President of Referee Operations / Director of Officials, Southeastern Conference Special Advisor Officiating Development & Performance, a Post-Traumatic Stress advocate, consultant, an author, a husband, a father, a son, a brother and many other titles. My journey has led to multiple transitions in life which have made me more of a complete human being.

Go out into the world and take control of your destiny, and remember to stay healthy, stay safe, and take care of each other!

# Introduction

# Journey into Discovery

> *"Your life is a story of transition. You are always leaving one chapter behind while moving on to the next."*
> **Anonymous**

"Transition" is a very common term to the average basketball player. When on defense, getting into transition is when you quickly gain possession of the ball and push the offense down to your basket as quickly as possible. You will often hear a coach screaming at their team urging them to get back on transition defense. Transition in the flow of a basketball game is as familiar to the average basketball player as the motion involved in brushing their teeth.

Mention transition in any other context and it can be a scary word. It is often associated with uncertainty and ambiguity. A transition occurs when you move from one home to another, or switch from job to job, or it can also mean shifting from one relationship to another.

Everybody goes through transitions in life. Babies transition from the womb to the outside world. Kids transition from toddler to youth to young adult to adult to "seasoned" adult, and ultimately, we all transition from life to death. Transitioning is a part of life, so we may as well embrace the journey.

*Adonal Foyle, MA, MBA*

There's one transition process that's especially difficult—the transition for a professional athlete out of a professional playing career. Take the example of a former international basketball player, Alexus Foyle, who is a cousin of mine. When I asked about his retirement experience, he talked about how difficult the journey was, claiming "It was pretty tough. I still have my moments because I still feel like I can play at a high level. So it was really, really tough for me to hang it up and tell myself that I had to stop playing. I felt like I had a lot left in my tank, and also felt like I didn't get my full value out of playing basketball. I was always underpaid and I wanted to keep on going to reach that high level. But at the same time, I was getting older, and once I started watching my age, I realized I wasn't going to get a proper job in basketball. I said to myself, 'Shit, I have to let it go.' So it's hard."

When professional athletes walk away from their sport, it is usually not their choice. The decision is made because they can no longer perform at the highest level due to one or more factors, including injury, age, and/or de-selection. Very rarely do players get the privilege of walking away from the game on their own terms. But even those who do walk away on their own terms don't always have a plan in place for their post-playing career.

For most players, the transition to life after their professional sport is uncharted territory. For much of their lives, they've spent countless hours working on their craft—throwing a thousand more football passes, taking a thousand more three-point jumpers, or taking a thousand more baseball swings than any other player. That is what has made them stand out. If you have been an athlete for most of your life, you've been primarily known simply as an athlete. But the fact is, playing sports is just one chapter in your entire book of life.

Most of the time, players don't think beyond their playing days because of the belief that they'll be able to play forever—a very strong belief among athletes. This self-fulfilling prophecy of believing that your career will never end hinders the athletes' ability to adequately prepare for the work involved and carve out a meaningful life beyond their sport. Often they stick to the game longer than they should because they haven't thought about what they will do next. Examples include: Bob Cousy, George Mikan, Magic Johnson, Rasheed Wallace, and Michael Jordan. I believe that part of their extended carrers are due to their competitive restless souls. At the same time, another reason is the clarity of purpose they get from playing their sport. And in many ways, the structure and control they have over their sports is a powerful draw to keep them attached to the profession.

Transition means a lot more than simply figuring out what to do once it's time to hang it up. It's about the necessary steps athletes need to take in order to begin earning income again. Even more importantly, it's about finding a sense of purpose and meaning in their life—not just sitting at home all day with nothing to do, or falling back on a job they don't have the motivation for or find unsatisfying.

The truth is, nothing can fully replace playing with (and against) some of the best athletes in the world in front of tens of thousands of fans. When athletes walk away from the game, they need to appreciate how difficult it will be to fill that void. Everyone has to figure out a path to find their new career or craft. They may want to stay in the game, but in another capacity such as coaching, becoming a front office executive or becoming a color commentator (nationally or locally). Is starting a business the right path? Perhaps creating a non-profit organization? Does it make sense to go back to school to finish that degree? There are many options available to players, but it is up to them to decide what makes the most sense for their personal journey.

In 2015, I wrote a book called "Winning the Money Game," which highlighted the plight of professional athletes who lost the money they earned during their professional careers. Much of

*Adonal Foyle, MA, MBA*

their financial problems and strain was the result of their not being prepared for the transition process.

In this book, I focus on transition by providing tools and key takeaways that can help people in all walks of life—but especially professional athletes—achieve a successful transition.

After reading this book, you will understand what is involved as well as the difficulty of transition, and why most players don't start planning until it's too late. I hope this will raise awareness and help everyone think about and have that uncomfortable conversation about transition well before their own transition process actually begins.

This book is not about telling you what is the right path or wrong path when transitioning into a new career. We are all in the same boat because we are all trying to find happiness. This book is about letting you know that transition is a process, and the process comes in waves. Transition itself is different for everybody. Some might stay in one stage longer than another, some might breeze right through. But what I know for sure is that we all have to go through the process, and we have to be dedicated to it if we want to be set up for success. We have to understand that change is about finding a combination of things that bring you happiness. That's what is most important.

My objective is to make everyone aware of the tools necessary to get through the process successfully. Moving forward, I will be using references such as *he*, *his* and *him*, but this is for all athletes, regardless of gender, who compete at a high level and need tools to transition from one life phase to another.

After I have explored professional athletes' transitions, I will share interviews I have conducted with other people undergoing transitions and briefly compare their experiences with those of athletes. I have talked with former military personnel who have transitioned out of the military and into civilian life. Additionally I interviewed people transitioning out of regular 9-5 jobs.

*Winning the Transtioin Game*

I myself have thought a great deal about the process of transition—as far back as when I was still playing. But transitioning out of pro sports was still a far more difficult thing to go through than I expected. My own experience embodies the phrase, "easier said than done."

But before I begin to share my transition experience, it's important to understand how I reached that point.

The journey begins...

# PART I:

# REALITY

# Chapter One

# The Faces of Transition

*"Life is pleasant. Death is peaceful. It's the transition that's troublesome."*

**Isaac Asimov**

On August 17, 2010, I announced my retirement from the NBA by writing this poem:

LOVE SONG TO A GAME

How should I tell thee goodbye?

What can you say about a love affair to rival that of Romeo & Juliet? This is not just some melancholy ode to a hackneyed love of mortals.

I found our love deep in the entrails of the Caribbean Sea. Love that swept me to a land where our embrace became mythical.

You showed me a world that few have dreamt of.

Colgate's golden steeple, a sojourn where ancient teachings flooded my mind.

*Adonal Foyle, MA, MBA*

*There in the Chenango Valley where 13 sang my soul to flight, basketball laid siege to my soul.*

*I do not cry for the passing of our love for it stands radiant while my brittle bones crumble through swift time.*

*I have known you by so many faces; I will spend my end of days recalling.*

*You have infected so many with the allure of riches and black gold. But I am not angry with you my love. For to a boy who was lost in the bosom of nothing you gave hope and a home.*

*Like the flickering of a light we come and go without much fuss. So I leave you to fend off seekers, hoping they too will cherish your unyielding countenance.*

*As for me, I will forever live in the glare of your loving embrace. From time to time I hope you will look in on this pitiful fool.*

*I will miss brothers of a quilt struggling with burning lights. If I offer advice, pierce beyond the glaring lights and see the faces behind the wall. Don't be fooled by the magician's nimble fingers. For this is a life with mirrors and screens. Its only truth lies in the understanding it will all end.*

*The sound I will take home is the symphony of thousands of screaming friends.*

*Warriors, Magic and yes, Memphis too, I sing you praise, hope, blessings,*

*Flowing from a boy's songs of thanks to you and you and you, to all I knew.*

*Please stay my "immortal love."*

    I was very fortunate to be able to walk away from my professional basketball career on my own terms. At least that was the brave face I put on for the 2009-10 season. Prior to the start of the season, coming off an appearance in the 2009 NBA Finals with the Orlando Magic, I was training in Los Angeles with my teammate Dwight Howard. At 34 years old, and with over 10 years of NBA service under my belt, I was feeling great. I could still hang with one of the top players in the league and I was excited about the possibility of making another run at an NBA championship. Jumper after jumper, I was hitting shots over Dwight, who was the reigning Defensive Player of the Year at the time. I could see how irritated he was becoming that this "old man" still had some game in him.

Then, I attempted a high fadeaway shot over him and—POP—my knee went out!

I came crashing down... and with it my NBA career. At this point I was entering my 13th season. I had already undergone multiple surgeries on my knees. I've had my fair share of other injuries over the years as well, but when I heard my knee pop, I knew instantly this was the end. I laid on the ground until my manager came to my aid.

"I'm done," I kept saying over and over.

I flashed back to the very first game I ever played in the NBA. I remember feeling so excited to see my friends and family after the game in 1997. Among them was my adoptive father, Jay Mandle. I was waiting for him to tell me how proud he was, but instead he asked what sounded to me like a random question: "This is great Adonal. But what do you think you are going to do with the rest of your life?" I had no idea where this was coming from. I was 22 years old and I had my entire NBA career ahead of me. But my father always talked about suffering from what he called anticipatory anxiety—worrying about what was next. Further he was and will always be a teacher for life with an uncanny ability to ask very important leading questions. As a professor of economics, Jay was quite aware of the

## Adonal Foyle, MA, MBA

trends regarding the difficulties athletes have in transition when their pro career ends. He knew the social science literature from psychology, history, and sociology. I would not be surprised if he had engaged in some forecasting, making predictions about my future in basketball based on analysis of past and current data.

Now, after my career-ending injury, his question was the very one I began asking myself.

Before my injury, I had studied at John F. Kennedy University in Pleasant Hill, California for a master's degree in sport psychology. For my thesis on retirement of professional athletes, I spoke to a dozen former athletes, soliciting their views. This of course gave me some ideas of what to expect once I retired.

But on that day in LA, writhing in pain on the gym floor, worries about my future were at the forefront. The truth was, I did not have a plan in place.

I remained on the Orlando Magic roster during the 2009-10 season, but started that year wearing street clothes on the bench. However, I was in complete denial about whether I would ever play again.

After yet another knee surgery, I started talking to myself: "I'm not ready to hang it up just yet. But if you can give me one more good year to play, I'll be better prepared to walk away next season."

But my knee wasn't listening to me. I suited up for a handful of games, but I never got to play. As much as I denied it, the truth was that I just couldn't play. The blast of the horn after the end of each game propelled me yet another step closer to retirement and the start of a post-NBA career. But I really had no idea what that career was going to be.

Here are the views of other professional athletes, talking about their own transitions:

*Winning the Transition Game*

**Vontae Davis**: *Career Highlights* Davis played cornerback for the Miami Dolphins, Indianapolis Colts, and Buffalo Bills of the NFL and a two-time Pro Bowler, was involved in one of the most extraordinary retirement scenarios in professional sports.

*Retirement Highlights* He hung up his football cleats and walked away from the game at halftime. Davis elaborated on his retirement discussion in *The Undefeated* that "Leaving was therapeutic, bro, I left everything the league wanted me to be, playing for my teammates while injured, the gladiator mentality, it all just popped. And when it popped, I just wanted to leave it all behind. So that's why I don't care what people say. That experience was personal and not meant for anyone else to understand. It was me cold turkey leaving behind an identity that I carried with me for so long. I went to the bench after that series and it just hit me, I don't belong on that field anymore."

**Al Iafrate**: *Career Highlights* The former NHL defenseman is most famous for his rocket slap shot that set the NHL Skills Competition record, which stood for 16 years, at 105.2 miles per hour (169.3 km/h). He was the fourth pick in 1984 NHL draft by the Toronto Maple Leafs.

*Retirement Highlights* Iafrate states, "It's hard to replace the passion you have for a sport. There aren't many jobs that you retire from where you get to prove that you are the very best of the best in front of thousands and thousands of people every night."

**Shaun Livingston:** *Career Highlights* Shaun Livingston is a three-time NBA champion who played with NBA teams. In a 15 year professional career, Livingston played 959 games for nine teams. He won three NBA championships as a Golden State Warrior—in 2015, 2017 and 2018. On his way to the NBA, Shaun racked up quite a resumé including, McDonald's All-American (2004), First-team Parade All-American (2004), Fourth-team Parade All-American (2003) and Illinois Mr. Basketball.

*Retirement Highlights* In 2019 Shaun announced his retirement on Instagram saying, "After 15 years in the NBA, I'm excited, sad, fortunate and grateful all in one breath. Hard to put into a caption all of the emotions it takes to try and accomplish your dreams. I wasn't supposed to be here. Anybody that has beat the odds understands the mental and emotional strain it takes to inspire yourself on an uphill war, let alone inspire others. 'The injury' gave me a chance to find and prove to myself (and the world) that I wouldn't be defined by my circumstances. With my time in the League what I will be most proud of is the fact that my character, values and faith were tested, and I persevered."

**Deion Sanders:** *Career Highlights* Former MLB and NFL superstar; member of Pro Football Hall of Fame, two-time Super Bowl winner, perennial all-pro and one of only two people in NFL history to score a touchdown six different ways (interception return, punt return, kickoff return, receiving, rushing, and a fumble recovery).

*"Most guys don't understand that playing the game is only what you do, it's not who you are."*
**Deion Sanders**

*Retirement Highlights* In a Forbes article Sanders shared an insightful take on transition: "Most guys don't understand that playing the game is only what you do, it's not who you are. Players who fall in love with the game get heartbroken because the sport doesn't have a heart or the ability to love you back."

**Peyton Manning:** *Career Highlights* The All-Pro quarterback devoted 18 years to the NFL, 14 years with the Colts and, after receiving neck surgery, spent his last four with the Broncos until retiring after winning Super Bowl 50. Manning is the only starting quarterback to win Super Bowl titles for two franchises. He is decorated in several records, including the NFL's All-Time Leader in passing touchdowns.

*Retirement Highlights* Manning was able to exit his career on a high note that most athletes who go under intensive surgery do not get to experience. In his retirement speech Manning stated, "Football has taught me not to be led by obstructions and setbacks but instead to be led by dreams. Due to some good genes, I'm smart enough to know that those lessons can enrich who I am and where I go from here." He continued, "I'm totally convinced that the end of my football career is just the beginning of something I haven't even discovered yet. Life is not shrinking for me; it's morphing into a whole new world of possibilities."

**Ruthie Bolton:** *Career Highlights* Seven-year WNBA player, Two-Time Olympic Gold Medalist, All-Star player for the WNBA's Sacramento Monarchs, over 2,000 career points, 4th all-time on the WNBA three-point list, created the Aim High Program, first WNBA player to have her number retired, and member of the Women's Basketball Hall of Fame.

*Retirement Highlights* "My transition was hard, because I wasn't given the opportunity to retire. In my last season, I was cut from the team. Not too many people know that. It was the hardest thing in the world for me. After everything I've done for my team, I felt betrayed. I had to do a lot of self-evaluating. What do I do now? This hurt me so bad. But I knew there was something bigger for me out there. I just didn't know what that was at the time. The organization did offer me a job in the front office. I had three weeks to think about it. But at the time, I was just lost. I didn't know what to do. I realized that I didn't want to live a life of resentment. Sometimes you become a prisoner of your own emotions. So I decided to take the job.

My first game back as a member of the front office, the crowd went crazy when they saw me. That was closure to me. Because I had the chance to say goodbye. When players leave the game, sometimes there's a feeling of losing your identity. Who are you if you're not a player anymore…especially when it comes to the way you exit. It wasn't on my terms so it was like a wound that couldn't heal. I needed to think about how to heal this wound. So when I heard the crowd, that lifted me up. They really helped me with my transition.

I'm really glad I stayed with the organization. The fans saved me. I stayed involved with the game, I got to meet so many people. And now, in my new position – working in fan development for the Sacramento Kings – I found a new identity. Before games, I would meet with fans, chat with them about what they think is going to happen during the game that night. Eventually, I was getting a lot of requests for appearances. The more appearances I made, the more I started to heal. That actually became a bridge for what became my new career. I wrote a book. I became a motivational speaker and I started the Aim High program as a way to help young people overcome adversity."

During my research for this book, I interviewed many retirees. From those interviews four macro-themes emerged and each element refers to a different section of this book.

The four unique experiences of transition are:

- Ambivalence
- Searching
- Anxiety
- Epiphany

At the end of the book, I will offer some lessons and takeaways, as well as some additional interviews with professional athletes and others.

# Chapter Two

# Phase 1: Ambivalence

*"I was happy that the Orlando Magic organization offered me a position in the front office (I am the new Director of Player Development). I didn't give much thought about working in basketball in my post-playing days; but this was as close to the game as I could get and still feel like I'm contributing to the team. The first few days on the job, I felt really excited about my new role. But something hit me on the way to the training room. I couldn't go in. I refused to set foot in the locker room because I knew that if I went in there, I would have to deal with the fact that I really was retired. So for the first three weeks I simply refused to enter the locker room."*

—Adonal Foyle, MA, MBA  Journal entry:  September 27, 2010
**exactly one month after retirement**

There are two moments in a professional athlete's career when his life will literally change overnight. The first moment is Draft Night, when he gets hired as a professional athlete for the first time. After putting in countless hours asking parents for rides to practice, eating and sleeping the sport, playing games, traveling to different cities for camps and more games—all the way from AAU to college—the hard work finally pays off when your name is announced by the league commissioner. You're drafted! One snap of the fingers and suddenly a player is a pro and earning more money than he could possibly imagine.

The second moment is the very first day he realizes he is no longer a professional athlete. No more practice days. No more games. No more hitting the road to hang out with teammates. No more playing in front of 20,000 screaming fans. No longer is he among the top athletes in the world in his sport. No "professional athlete" job title. No more special perks because of his baller status. He is simply back to being a private citizen.

The initial experience of many of the people I interviewed about this second moment—the moment of retirement—was one of ambivalence. Many of them had mixed feelings and sometimes even contradictory attitudes about their initial retirement experience. Taken together, the range of reactions of the athletes I interviewed were so diverse that I refer to the overall experience as one of ambivalence. The emotions of these athletes when they were facing the end of their professional careers included excitement about spending time with their families, the desire to try something new, relief from the constant injuries and pain they endured, concern about shedding their athlete title, and feelings of liberation from escaping the structure and rigor of sports.

Some of them were never actually able to come to grips with what has happened. One athlete I talked to about his retirement was five years removed from the game. But when I asked about his retirement, he corrected me, saying that he was not retired at all, but waiting for the call from a general manager so he could return to playing. That call of course never came.

For others, there are aspects of retirement that bring newly retired athletes pure joy. For starters, no more practices. There probably are

a few players out there who enjoy practice, but my bet would be if you ask ten players if they liked to practice, you may get a yes from two or three—at most. After all, most practices are long, tedious and boring. *What are we talking about? Practice? We're talking about practice, man."*
**Allen Iverson, 2013**

No more practice also means no more diet restrictions. Suddenly, you can eat whatever your heart desires—year-round. And perhaps best of all, there are no more people to report to at certain times of the day. No coaches yelling at you during practice for throwing a lazy pass. No more general managers to say "yes, sir" to, and no more PR people making you stay late in the locker room answering questions you don't want to answer. You feel that you are finally free!

Kristi Yamaguchi, who won an Olympic Gold Medal in figure skating in 1992, was ultimately able to carve out a lucrative professional career in retirement. She remembers the feeling of euphoria when first leaving the sport and the freedom that came with it. But she found out that it was only a short time before reality set in.

"That first month of 'normalcy' was kind of liberating," she said. "I felt like 'Wow, I don't have to worry about what I'm eating, how much sleep I get, or about training every day.' For a moment, it felt like I was going to be on vacation for the rest of my life. But you do get to a point where you need a purpose."

Some athletes leave their sport because of injuries or family concerns. Mark Munoz was one of those athletes. This former UFC fighter wasn't always involved in mixed martial arts. In fact, he started out as an All-American wrestler in both high school and college. After graduating from Oklahoma State University, he coached wrestlers at UC Davis, where he met a fellow wrestler-turned MMA fighter, Uriah Faber. Uriah introduced Mark to MMA, and Munoz ultimately became one of the top middleweight fighters in the world. When he finally chose to walk away from his sport, he stated "Throughout my whole career, I had been dealing with injuries. I broke little bones here and there. I have scars everywhere. And scars tell the story. Toward the end of my career, I cut a lot of weight. The most I ever lost in a fight was 75 pounds in 12 weeks. But my career has always been like that—the ups and downs in weight, even when I was wrestling in high school. I would weigh 225 to 245 pounds and I would cut it down to 180. Sometimes I would get a six-week notice that I needed to cut down on weight. So I would go through these ups and downs. Because of that, my body started taking a toll. To this day, I still feel like my body is taking a toll from that."

Just as Mark had to make the transition from a wrestler to a MMA fighter, the time eventually came for him to transition out of his fighting career—while still at the top of his game. Injuries started to become more common for Mark, even though he was close to having a title shot before he walked away from the ring. In Mark's moving retirement speech, he said to the crowd, "You might get hit by unforeseen things like cancer or diabetes but your life doesn't stop there—you get back up and keep competing to the best of your ability. That's what my career has been about." But for Mark, it was more than the injuries that forced him to walk away from his sport. He was also missing his family, and especially his son's life.

Mark remembered vividly:

"One day, my son told me that he wanted to quit soccer and baseball and focus on wrestling. I asked him why. He was so good at soccer and baseball and I just asked him why he would want to quit those sports to take up wrestling. He said he loved wrestling and he has a passion for it. I told him that he would have to cut weight, he might get hurt a lot. He didn't have to worry about that stuff in soccer and baseball. But he was committed to wrestling. So I started to ask him what his goals were. He wanted a full-ride scholarship to a Division I university. At this time, he's in the eighth grade. I started asking him 'Why are you thinking about this now?' Right now, there are 72 Division I colleges that offer full-ride scholarships in wrestling. There are tens of thousands of kids who want that scholarship. I asked him 'What makes you think that out of the tens of thousands of kids who want a full-ride scholarship to a Division I school, that you'll be able to get one?' Without batting an eye, he looks at me and says 'I got you, Dad.' That hit me in the chest so hard. That was the straw that broke the camel's back. That's when I decided I was done. So six weeks before my last fight, I announced that I was going to retire. I wanted to be there for my family. I was sitting back and watching my wife be a superwoman. She was shuttling the kids here and there, taking care of the house. And she was running my gym. I'm sure it was crazy for her. So I knew it was time. I could take care of these injuries. But time was fleeting. I can't get time back. At the time, I had a daughter who was going to leave the house in two years. Fast forward to four years later, my son now has that full-ride scholarship, my daughter is in college, and my two younger kids are on their way to doing the same thing. Now, looking back, I could see the benefits of me retiring because I see my family benefitting from it."

Most players don't think that the identity they embraced as a professional athlete is an albatross around their neck. But the further athletes get away from the game, the more they realize that they have so much identity wrapped up in their sport that it becomes both painful and difficult to shed.

But one retired athlete, Andy Roddick, a celebrated tennis player, was able to shed his athletic identity without a backward glance. After he retired, he took the extreme measure of throwing away most of his trophies. Roddick was quoted as saying, "These don't mean success to me, they don't define me and I don't really care to have these material things sitting around the house." He probably just wanted to look toward the future and shed the identity that he had in the sports world.

> *It's imperative to have a plan in place so that players can walk away from the game knowing that there is a concrete career plan to look forward to.*

Professional sports are unusual in the sense that athletes are deemed experts in their respective fields. The problem is that while an athlete spends all his life becoming an expert in this field, that expertise may be useful only for a mere four years, maybe less. It's true that some NBA players have a long professional life—a few can even play well into their 40s. Vince Carter, after playing 22 NBA seasons, retired after the abbreviated 2019-2020 season. However, it's very difficult to experience that kind of longevity as a professional athlete. But even 40-year-olds have plenty of life to live. So it's imperative to have a plan in place so that players can walk away from the game knowing that there's a concrete career plan to look forward to.

Each player will reach a certain point in his post-playing career when he finally realizes that he is no longer an active professional athlete. For some players, it may be the day after the end of the season. For others, it's not until summer is over and they realize they don't have to report to training camp. Others don't come to the true realization until much later—even years. It's different for each player in terms of how he experiences transition. But for many, all of a sudden they realize that they have no idea who they are anymore, and they have no idea what to do next.

Part of how well athletes handle their transition depends on whether they were able to take care of their finances while still active in the league. Chris Dudley, who played 16 years in the NBA, became a financial advisor and is currently the Director of Sports and Entertainment at Boston Private Wealth. In an opinion piece, Dudley laid out the states for athletes who faced the plight of going through financial hardship: "For most athletes, there is no easy fix for a significant financial setback. Unlike virtually every other profession out there, an athlete's career earnings are compressed into just a handful of years. Time is not on the side of those who are undisciplined, unrealistic or too trusting. Careers are short, and savings must last for the rest of your life. Beating the odds requires a lot of work and discipline."

The former NBA big man, who played 886 games across 16 years in the NBA, argued that:

"At last look, an estimated 60 percent of former NBA players go broke within five years of departing the league. And by no means are these financial problems confined to the NBA. A reported 78 percent of former NFL players have gone bankrupt or under financial stress just two years after retirement." (Dudley, 2018)

If athletes leave the game not having managed their money well, or if they left school early and never went back to get a degree, the question of what to do upon retirement is really scary. However if they created and maintained a discipline concerning their spending habits, saving and investing, chances are their transition will go much smoother. For many, one of the worst aspects of transition is that they go deeply into debt.

*"I had to limit my expenses and be more mindful of where my money was going."*

One way or another, reality sets in. And it's at that time that the athlete begins to think seriously about what his next move should be. For me, despite the fact that my injury ultimately forced me to retire, I did the best I could to retire on my own terms. But after the smoke cleared, I began to think, "Now what?" I spent a month trying to figure out what I could do next. My first priority was to finish my master's degree in sport psychology. After that, I knew that I had to look for a job, but I had to really think about what I wanted to do. And third, I had to know my financial constraints, because even though I made a good deal of money as an NBA player, I was no longer making that kind of money as a retired player. I had to limit my expenses, be more mindful of where my money was going, and carefully consider before moving ahead with any financial investments or business moves.

The fallacy is that retired NBA players and other professional athletes with high salaries believe they can live off their accumulated wealth and never have to work again. But the stark truth is that many NBA players go broke or experience financial distress within the first five years of retirement as the above statistic states. They simply don't have the tools necessary to adapt to a lifestyle different from when they were playing—income is no longer coming in, yet expenditures stay the same. This is too true of athletes in other sports as well. Furthermore, most professional athletes believe that their leagues did little to help them deal with these kinds of issues while they were players or after retirement.

Brent Jones, who played 13 seasons in the NFL with the San Francisco 49ers, won three Super Bowls during his career. He shared with me how leagues such as the NFL have done a less-than-admirable job in preparing players for the next phase of their lives.

"To be honest," said Brent, "I think the leagues do a horrible job of preparing guys. They never ask them, 'What can you do next?' or 'What skills have you developed throughout your life that can help you transition into your next career, whether it's business, charity work, media or something else you're passionate about? None of the leagues prepare their players. I find there's no real concern or effort to prepare guys for their post-career. Maybe the NBA will take the lead, but I've talked to the NFL multiple times over the years. They'll tell you in a meeting setting that successful transition is important to them. But they really don't care because ex-athletes are no longer generating revenue for the current league. It's PR, basically, because they're not really concerned."

*Do not underestimate the importance of preparation while you are still active in the league.*

So if a player hasn't thought about making preparations for life after professional sports, he's virtually on his own. It's easy to fall into the mindset that worrying about a post-sports career can wait until after retirement. Theoretically, an athlete might believe he has generated enough income during the course of his career and that will allow him plenty of time and resources to think about a second career. But, while it is true the more money you have, the longer you can give yourself to find a new job, do not underestimate the importance of preparation while you are still active in the league.

For some athletes, retirement is extremely painful. Former NBA player Marc Jackson, one of my teammates at Golden State, played nine seasons in the league. He grossed nearly $25 million in the NBA and continued his career by playing overseas. By the time he retired, he was financially set. But because he did not have a second career planned, he initially faced boredom, which put him in a difficult situation before he eventually found a path that worked for him.

"It's very important to think about your next career while you're still playing," Marc told me. "I was one of those guys who really didn't want to start planning a new career because when I signed my contract, I thought I was set for life. When I finally retired, I told myself I CANNOT get bored! I have to keep my mind occupied because you get in trouble when you get bored. So if you have nothing on your mind as far as planning your next career, things start to happen." Marc continued, "You start spending more of your money, you start doing stupid things because your mind is idling in neutral."

Mark further explains, "The most common emotions you feel are fear and laziness. We are all born lazy and we're all going to be lazy. But we are also fearful of failure so we don't want to try things which, in turn, makes us lazy again. With those things in mind, if you can't find something that will stimulate you to move forward—not necessarily what makes you money, but what makes you happy—your mind will go berserk. Things will happen out of nowhere. Relationships will be ruined with friends, with family, and with your spouse. It will be disastrous because your mind is just sitting there doing nothing."

Many players feel the same way Marc did when it comes to walking away from the game and the struggles that come with that transition. Regardless of the sport—hockey, football, baseball, track & field, volleyball, basketball, cricket, soccer, rugby, mixed martial arts, boxing, swimming, figure skating or any sport in between—there is one truth: the opportunity to compete at a high level will eventually come to an end, and, sadly many are unprepared to do anything else.

The end of a professionial athlete's playing career means that he has come to a crossroad in his life. He will wonder what he is going to do for the rest of his life. Someone who is 33 or 34 years old may be considered over the hill in professional sports, but in reality, someone that age still has his whole life in front of him. According to Bleacher Report, the average career lifespan of an NBA player is just over four years. Other sports are similar: the average career lifespan of an NFL player is 3.5 years, while the average for an NHL player is 5.5 years, and the average for a Major League Baseball player is 5.6 years. For an NBA player, his career could potentially be done by the time he's 26 years old or even younger.

Then what?

What makes a professional athlete's transition so difficult is the intensity and difficulty it takes to make it to the professional ranks in the first place, and to remain at the top of his sport. Single-mindedness and all-consuming effort are needed to not only make it to that level but also to stay at the top. This type of tunnel vision is a big part of the reason it is so difficult for professional athletes to walk away from the game.

There are about 30,000 professional athletes worldwide who get paid to play a sport. Here are some reflections of those who took the plunge into retirement.

> **Annika Sörenstam:** *Career Highlights* Won 72 official LPGA tournaments including 10 majors and 18 other tournaments internationally. She was the first woman to play in a PGA Tour event since 1945.
>
> *Retirement Highlights* Annika told Forbes, "My heart and body were telling me that it was time to move on. I had won the US Open and several other championships. I had climbed my Mount Everest and the view was beautiful from the top but it was time for me to climb other mountains and see other peaks in my life."

> **Shannon Miller:** *Career Highlights* At the time, the most decorated American gymnast, male or female, in history before Simone Biles took the crown in 2016. Two silver and three bronze medals at the 1992 Olympics and she led the "Magnificent Seven" to the US Women's first ever Team Gold, capturing gold on the balance beam in 1996.
>
> *Retirement Highlights* "I didn't know how to be a regular person. After I retired, I initially watched a lot of TV, gaining four dress sizes on my five-foot frame. It was very disheartening but it helped me realize that I had to find my next passion in life."

**Andrew Luck:** *Career Highlights* Four-time NFL Pro Bowl quarterback played all seven years of his professional career with the Indianapolis Colts. He has earned multiple honors and awards throughout his professional career.

*Retirement Highlights* Andrew announced his retirement before the start of the 2019 football season. Luck said he just could not play football anymore because of the mounting injuries. Over the course of his career, Luck's injuries included torn cartilage in two ribs, a partially torn abdomen, a lacerated kidney that left him peeing blood, one concussion, a torn labrum in his throwing shoulder, and calf and ankle issues. With a mounting listing of physical trauma, Luck retired, saying, "I haven't been able to live the life I want to live.... It's taken the joy out of this game. The only way forward for me is to remove myself from football and this cycle I've been in." He continued, "I'm in pain, I'm still in pain, I've been in this cycle for four years.... I don't feel like I can live the life I want moving forward." Finally, he argued that, "The lack of progress just builds up and you turn the corner and run into another stumbling block."

**Kris Draper:** *Career Highlights:* Four-time Stanley Cup champion, a Frank J. Selke Trophy winner, scored over 100 goals with the Detroit Red Wings and was a member of the famous Grind Line.

*Retirement Highlights* Kris tells Forbes, "Hockey was such a part of my life, as well as my family's, that I knew we were all going to miss it. For the first few weeks my son was in tears. 'I miss you being a Red Wing, Daddy.' I didn't know what to say, so we just cried together. Nobody prepares you for that kind of stuff. What I did to prepare in a practical way was after taxes, I always tried to save at least 50% of my game checks."

**Brian McCann**: *Career Highlights:* Played MLB for the Atlanta Braves, New York Yankees, and Houston Astros. Was a seven-time All-Star, a six-time Silver Slugger Award winner, and won the 2017 World Series with the Astros.

*Retirement Highlights* McCann retired after 15 years in Major League Baseball. He told reporters "This is it for me... I'm going to go home and be a dad and play with those kids."

**Sharon Ann Cohen:** *Career Highlights:* Sharon worked 34 years in the insurance marketing field with the last 23 with Aon, a brokerage company, rising from a marketing manager to a senior vice president, and leading a team of 40 creative folks. She crafted strategy, built plans, created campaigns, managed events and excelled at managing people and making things happen.

*Retirement Highlights* Sharon claims that "it was time for me to look around and see that the joy of living was simply being sucked out of me. I was feeling overwhelmed, dragging myself to work, out of shape, heavy and unhappy...not my natural state. The treadmill of life was wearing me out. Retirement beckoned."

She continued, "I read a lot of books on retirement, how to follow your passion, etc. but none of them spoke to me like *Younger Next Year for Women*, by Chris Crowley and Henry S. Lodge, M.D. So I transitioned all the successful work habits into working at being in motion six days a week for the rest of my life...and I feel wonderful."

> **Ana Julaton:** *Career Highlights:* A Filipino-American professional boxer and mixed martial artist, WBO Super Bantamweight World Champion and IBA Super Bantamweight World Champion.
>
> *Retirement Highlights* Announcing her retirement on social media, she wrote that "As a competitor inside the ring and cage, I'm confident in leaving the sport of Boxing and MMA fully knowing there are so many wonderful, passionate, and hardworking women who continue to carry the torch as a guiding light for the bright future of our arena." When I sat down with Ana for an interview about her transition, she said "I felt like my prime ended in 2013. But because of the slow movement in opportunities that were there for me, I just needed to see if I could still do it. I needed to know. But it eventually hit me when my body just didn't want to train anymore. I was done. The idea of wanting to hurt someone, it just got really old. And, naturally, you would just be an evil person if all you wanted to do was hurt someone for the rest of your life."
>
> When asked about what she was going to do in the next phase of her life she had a list. "First, I plan to catch up with everyone in my family. But I also need to catch up with myself. Being able to step out of my own tunnel vision makes me feel good. I feel grounded. I've been thinking about writing a book and possibly doing some commentary work and talking about the sport. I definitely want to perpetuate everything that I've learned and work with the next generation of fighters. I also just want to promote healthy living. It's important to exercise, eat right and make it a way of life. Learn to be happy and live life on your own terms despite what the world tries to tell you."

To be clear, not all athletes experience this stage of transition as voluntary because of career-ending injuries like the numerous knee injuries experienced by Portland Trail Blazers point guard Brandon Roy, or the blood clot condition of Miami Heat Chris Bosh, forcing him away from the game. Or like Jay Williams, the promising point guard, whose motorcycle crash ended his career, or Houston Rockets big man Yao Ming, whose toe forced him to end his career.

The initial stage of transition is characterized by a sense of confusion and ambivalence that is different for each athlete. Players experience a loss of identity, happiness about spending time with their families, relief at abandoning the restrictive structure of sport, relief from the pain and injury of sport, longing to continue their sporting career, the joy to eat what they want, and, finally, freedom from having to work out on demand.

This stage however is often short-lived because the very thing athletes have given up is the very thing that has provided them with purpose for many years. For most of them, the ambivalence stage quickly becomes the searching phase.

# Chapter Three
# Phase 2: Searching

*"Everyone has a plan... until they get punched in the mouth."*
**Mike Tyson**

In the above quote, former world heavyweight champion Mike Tyson was referring to his opponents who would spend weeks, if not months, training and watching film in preparation for their mega fight. Once Tyson landed that hard blow, much of that preparation went out the window for the opponent, and Tyson would collect another victory.

 *The searching phase involves figuring out what you can feel passionate about doing.*

In many ways, what happened to Tyson's opponents is similar to the transitions many professional athletes go through. Even for those who have a plan for their post-playing career, things don't always fall into place and they have to scramble to think of a Plan B. But the reality is that, for most players, there is no clear Plan B.

The searching phase involves figuring out what you can feel passionate about doing. The truth is, some people who don't have experiences beyond their sport may have to go back to school or learn a new trade in order to carve out a new path. Going back to school could be a new journey in itself because many athletes may have left school early. As was true of the first stage of transition, the searching phase is different for each player. He's now forced to think seriously about his next career. Even if he had thought about it as a player, at that point he would have likely approached it as a hobby. But when hit with the reality that it is time to find purpose, that player will feel pressured to find something very soon.

This searching phase is captured by former pitcher Tim Lincecum, who played Major League Baseball for the San Francisco Giants and the Los Angeles Angels. During a rare interview, from an article titled "Tim Lincecum hasn't formally retired yet, still trying to find his way" (2019), Tim said, "I'm trying to transition," and then continued outlining his predicament. "I think the hardest part was coming to grips with who I was after baseball, and I haven't even done it fully yet. I haven't formally retired. I'm not sure if I'm going to or not. So, with that, I'm just trying to find my way, going through a little bit of family stuff a few years ago, so that put perspective on things. Yeah, I'm just trying to find my way."

Players should know that the next career they choose may not necessarily be something they actually enjoy doing, even though it may be something they are good at. I encourage everyone to keep looking for something you are good at and also love doing. But at the same time, there is a misconception that work has to be something you enjoy 100%. The truth is not many people get the chance to do what they love 100% of the time. Where you are today is not where you are going to be tomorrow; sometimes it takes smaller steps to get to your ultimate goal.

Chris Bosh, a two-time NBA champion and 11-time NBA All-Star, had his career cut short by a blood clotting condition that the

NBA ruled to be a career-ending illness. Although Bosh's desire to continue playing was strong, he nevertheless had to announce his retirement in February 2019. In a recent interview, "Chris Bosh Talks about Getting a *Taste of Retirement*" (2107), he articulated the search phase he is currently in, claiming that he is trying "...to search for what I'm looking for. And I've come to some interesting conclusions. It's all about following my heart and what made me happy." Continuing on the path of self-discovery, he argued that "I'm still learning more about myself and my situation, and really off the court how to function there because I'm kind of getting the taste of retirement now.... Just trying to navigate those waters because it gets a little complicated sometimes.... Hoping one day that the stars align and I figure some things out and things kind of just go my way and I'll be able to do what I want to do. I don't know what that is yet."

Some athletes want to find a new career within their sport, especially if that's all they've known. Such careers can include becoming a coach, scout, TV analyst, or even a front office executive. But the truth is that there are only a limited number of those positions available within each sport. So if you decide to go that route, be prepared to do the work necessary to be very good at it. There will be both players and non-players out there who are gunning for the same positions.

Players must devote time to a lot of searching and a lot of evaluating to identify what they would like to do.

My own searching really began when I was let go as Director of Player Development for the Orlando Magic after two seasons in the front office. It was a move I wasn't anticipating, and I was left wondering what else was out there for me. Fortunately, I was in the middle of some writing projects, as well as pursuing my master's degree in sport psychology. But I considered them as projects and not so much as a second career. What was I going to do next? That was a question only I could answer.

*Adonal Foyle, MA, MBA*

Bret Hedican played in the National Hockey League for 18 seasons. He won a Stanley Cup with the Carolina Hurricanes and also represented Team USA twice for the U.S. Men's Hockey Team. Bret is also married to Olympic figure skater Kristi Yamaguchi.

 *The biggest thing for me is living in the moment and feeling the moment.*

Bret left the game a champion and an Olympian. And after playing at the highest level for nearly two decades, it wasn't easy to simply flip a switch. Bret emphasizes, "Everyone thinks that athletes can play golf and just go to the beach or whatever and relax. I realized quickly that that wasn't going to really satisfy 30 years of being driven. You start being driven at 10 years old and you don't shut that off. That faucet just keeps shooting water out of that hole. And now you're expected to turn the faucet off. That was very hard to do. The drive and goal-oriented mentality that I have is hard to turn off. The biggest thing for me is living in the moment and feeling the moment. To me, that is the biggest problem for athletes when they retire. When you're performing at your best, you have to stay in the moment. But all of a sudden, you retire and you forget all about that and you want to think about tomorrow and what's going to happen next week and next year. The 'what if's' set in very strong and it gets you into a lot of problems and a lot of trouble. If you start going back to all the things that made you a great player, and apply those things in life, that's a good start."

It took Bret a whole two years after retirement before reality set in that he was now a "former" NHL player. For some players like Bret and Kristi, because they have a partnership and children, they find that they have an opportunity to spend quality time that might have been scarce when they were athletes, often on the road. Thus their sense of purpose continued even while figuring out what's next in their career.

Bret was able to find a way to stay involved in the game that he loved in another way—but even that wasn't enough to fulfill him. "Kristi and I were doing an interview on the San Jose Sharks flagship TV station and I was approached to do pregame and postgame analysis for the Sharks," he said. "At first I said no, but Kristi thought I should do it. So she talked me into it, and that was really the godsend to get me out of the house. I'm going to San Jose and I'm watching the sport that I grew up and loved. I could talk about it and it wasn't that hard (although you do have to prepare, and you do have to be ready). But I thought that was a nice transition for me. It kept me around the game. And being around the game allowed me to do radio for the Sharks; it also helped me get involved with the U.S. Women's Hockey Team. And aside from that, I've started a couple of businesses that have helped me transition out."

"Seeing Bret go through this, and expressing his thoughts about it, I could tell that he needed to have a purpose when he woke up," Kristi interjected. "He needed to wake up knowing that he had something to do that day. In some ways, that first year, it seemed as if Bret had A.D.D. because he took on four jobs. How could he expect himself to be good at any of them when he's doing them all at the same time? I think Bret was so afraid of not having something to do that he started to overextend himself in other areas. He wanted to learn about one thing but looked at another area and said that was cool too. It would have been good if he had stuck to one thing—maybe two. And that's when he found the gig with the Sharks because he was able to talk about hockey again. I felt like after he retired, he was even more stressed out because he would worry about this, that or the other."

Bret was fortunate to have played as long as he had. He fulfilled his professional goal of winning a championship, and he generated enough income to take his time searching for his second career. Evidently, it wasn't that easy for him, as he went from one thing to another, searching for something that would fill the void when he left his sport as a player. But he did finally succeed.

## Adonal Foyle, MA, MBA

For many players, their playing careers end abruptly, and they are forced to suddenly think about their post-playing career. Roy "Zazu" Byrd, a very good friend of mine, had that experience and was not prepared for the searching he had to go through. Roy, who played five seasons with the Harlem Globetrotters, was a great ambassador for the organization. He is one of very few people who can say that he performed in front of both Nelson Mandela and Pope John Paul II. He got to travel the world, entertain millions of fans of all ages, and was making good money doing it. But a disagreement with the organization resulted in his leaving the team—and the game he loved—much sooner than he anticipated. While he had thoughts during his career about what he'd like to do once he was done playing, he never put a plan in motion. This left him vulnerable once he left the game.

"I had an idea of what I wanted to do once I retired, but I was not able to put my idea to use," he said. "I always wanted to dabble in the real estate market and buy properties and apartment buildings. Before I could do that, my career was cut short and I was forced into retirement so I was never able to dabble in the areas I wanted. That was my struggle."

With the feeling of having the rug pulled out from under him, Roy was not prepared for what life after basketball was going to look like. Roy used his basketball talents to entertain kids as a coach for basketball camps, but his anger toward the Globetrotters organization consumed him and prevented his planning for the future.

"I was on top of the world, and now I'm on the ground. That's not a happy place," Roy expressed. "I would make a big deal out of the smallest things because I was angry inside, and I would take it out on everyone else. Not a lot of people can make an easy transition. As a basketball player, you're in a different world. To come out of our world and go into a different world, it's not easy. I wasn't aware of all the new technologies in the world. Something as simple as that, I wasn't ready to because I was a ballplayer and all I knew was how to do was perform in front of fans and travel around the world. To just come home and sit there and think about what I was going to do next, and not having an answer to that question, it's easy to become an angry person."

When I retired in 2010, I was able to relate to some of Roy's concerns. While conducting research and interviewing players for this book, I learned many different perspectives when it comes to players and their struggles in transition. Roy and I talked a lot about the problems of transition, and we were able to help each other when it came to dealing with the unknown future after our professional careers.

I spoke with and interviewed a number of other athletes who, like Roy, were happy to voice their feelings. In fact, they seemed to welcome the chance to talk about their transitions after retirement. You can read more of those interviews in Chapter 8.

Transition may be tougher for those athletes who stayed in one place for a long time because they are less likely to have dealt with change. Regular people change jobs all the time, and even though athletes change teams, their vocation remains the same: playing at a professional level. For athletes transitioning out of sports into the "regular" world, it isn't just about changing jobs, it's about finding a completely new way of life and livelihood. I understand this shift all too well.

Since the average career span of an NBA player is a little more than four years, if a player reaches the pinnacle of his sport, then winds up walking away after such a short time, there are some adjustments that must be made. The shortened span makes the transition more intense. That's the realization we all must come to because of how much time we spent and invested to get to the professional level, but the return on our investment of time and effort isn't what we expected.

Transition is difficult for almost all professional athletes. We expected longevity. We expected injuries would happen to the 'other' guy. But we are often left high and dry. Stories abound about those who didn't handle their transition well.

The Searching stage as described above is characterized by a profound sense of being lost, and searching to find a replacement opportunity to fill the void left by the death of your career. This stage can take a long time and involve numerous trials and errors until the lucky ones actually find something that they like to do and that fits their skill set. Some can find what they would like to do, but may lack the confidence or skills to do the job which leads to further searching.

For many athletes, this stage leads to the anxiety stage. The majority of the following chapter is dedicated to the story of one particular player, not because I'm trying to make an example out of him, but because his experience is important and much more common among former professional athletes than most would like to admit.

# Chapter Four
# Phase 3: Anxiety

*"The interval between the decay of the old and the formation and establishment of the new constitutes a period of transition which must always necessarily be one of uncertainty, confusion, error, and wild and fierce fanaticism."*
**John C. Calhoun**

David Vaughn, son of a former NBA player, was a star forward coming out of high school. He was a member of USA Today's All-USA First Team in 1991 and attended the University of Memphis, where he averaged nearly a double-double from 1991 to 1995. He also played side-by-side with star player Anfernee Hardaway. Vaughn reunited with Hardaway in 1995 when he was drafted in the first round by the Orlando Magic, a team that was coming off an appearance in the NBA Finals. But David's story is ultimately one of great anxiety and struggle upon retirement.

Having been drafted in the first round meant guaranteed money for David, not to mention that he would be taken under the wings of players like Shaquille O'Neal and Horace Grant. Life was good for David and, in his mind, a long, lucrative career was in his future with an Eastern Conference powerhouse.

"I made hundreds of thousands of dollars," David told me. "I saved a few hundred thousand dollars. I had expensive houses, expensive cars."

> "When a guy comes into the NBA and signs a contract, he should be thinking about retirement." David Vaughn

Like most rookies, David fell victim to veteran players egging him on about playing the part of an NBA "baller" with a lot of money. They were telling him to get a better-looking car, and a bigger house. Shaq had told David to get rid of his Corvette because it was too small for a 6-foot-9 power forward and he could get seriously injured in an accident. David traded the Corvette, along with his first car (a GMC Yukon) for a Mercedes-Benz. After making an additional $70,000 in licensing fees due to using his likeness in video games, he bought a second car, a Range Rover 4.6. By the time he played his last game, he had purchased nine cars.

"When a guy comes into the NBA and signs a contract, he should be thinking about retirement," David said. "He should say things to himself like 'What am I going to do when I'm done playing basketball?' That wasn't my mindset when I was playing basketball. My mindset was 'I'm young, I'm healthy, and I'm going to be successful at this game.'"

David Vaughn's NBA career lasted four seasons.

He never got the tutelage he was looking for in Orlando from his star teammates. In fact, he played sparingly while with the Magic and was traded to Golden State during his second season as a pro, where he and I became teammates. But David left the Warriors after just four months in a trade to Chicago. He then spent his final season in the NBA with the New Jersey Nets, initially on a 10-day contract before signing on for the rest of the 1998-99 season.

David spent the rest of his career playing in Europe and finally hung it up in 2003. He was one of many who left the game prematurely due to de-selection. At the time, he had saved nearly $300,000 from the $2.2+ million in salary and moved back to Orlando. His $300,000 was pretty decent money by anyone's standards. But he was now a former NBA player who continued to live a lavish lifestyle as though he was still an active NBA player.

"I lived the fast life. I didn't think about retirement," he admitted to me. "I was thinking about basketball and *only* basketball. I wasn't thinking about anything else. Eventually, I wasn't making that same kind of money anymore. I had a wife and kids to support. The big eye-opener for me was that I had to go out and actually get a job."

David didn't have a plan in place for his post-playing career. And without a plan, much less an opportunity to immediately find work after basketball, he fell victim to mounting bills that he was unable to keep up with. He had home mortgages in Orlando and Nashville. He was forced to sell his home in Orlando and his Nashville home was auctioned off. The **anxiety** that was building up led to other issues between David and his family. By 2002, a year he refers to as the "lowest point" in his life, David faced domestic violence charges and began abusing drugs. Without a place to stay, he thought he could rely on his family, but they weren't there for him either.

"When my grandfather remarried, I thought I could go and stay with him at the house I grew up in," he recalled. "It was a lonely feeling to go from being a high school All-American, college All-American, being drafted in the NBA, and now I'm on the streets trying to make it on my own."

At one point, David admitted he was living in his truck. Without anyone to turn to, he relied heavily on his faith to draw strength.

"I was thinking, 'Lord, please don't leave me. I know you didn't bring me this far to let me go now.' It was a difficult feeling because

I had nowhere to turn," David remembers. "My mother passed away when I was 15 years old, and my father was struggling to take care of himself. I was basically left to make it on my own. There's a big homeless problem in this country. But I never thought it was going to happen to me."

David would also seek strength by reading books at libraries or bookstores. If he wasn't sleeping in his truck, he slept at hotels when he could afford to (or the Salvation Army when he had no money at all). Having a gym membership allowed him to not only work out but take showers and freshen up.

He did all he could to stay off the streets. Still struggling with drug abuse and unemployment, his luck turned for the worse when he was bitten by a brown recluse spider, sending him to the hospital. Bites from a brown recluse spider can form an ulcer that destroys soft tissue in the body. With mounting debt due to car payments, foreclosures, and now a hospital bill, David was transferred to a local nursing home.

His wife, who filed a restraining order after the domestic violence episode, ignored the order so she could care for him once she learned about his condition. Viewing his situation as a second chance at life, that moment appeared to be a turning point for David. Once he was healthy again, he moved back in with his wife. They had reconciled and David began to get back on his feet. Career-wise, however, he continued to struggle. During this time, he was laid off at a furniture store, where he had been working before he was hospitalized.

We often don't hear about a former athlete's struggles until it's too late. Oftentimes they will be in the news if they die, or if something else tragic happens. The truth is, there are too many stories similar to David's that we don't hear about because that particular player didn't make a big enough impact on the court to call attention to themselves in their post-playing career.

But David's story is just as important as that of a big-name player who lost his wealth and is without a skill or trade to fall back on. Reading stories like David's should be a constant reminder that there *are* resources out there for players to access in order to help them transition to their next career. It is people like David that I'm concerned about; he is the reason why I feel a call to action is necessary. There is absolutely no reason why players can't have a fulfilling career after sports. They just need to know that they can ask for help and that there are resources out there to assist them—such as this book.

A significant underpinning of the anxiety of transition is dealing with uncertainty. At its core, transition is about coming to terms with uncertainty and being the true neophyte that you are. As you begin to grow confident in your new space, you become less anxious. You reaffirm to yourself that you can adapt to your new world. There are days you can (and will) go backwards. The truth is many retired people experience depression, sadness, frustration and uncertainty as part of the retirement experience. They must often go through these feelings in order to create, develop and implement a post-career strategy.

For me, all I was thinking at the time was that I needed a job immediately after my post-playing career. Working in the Orlando Magic front office kept me around the lives of basketball players. It gave me something to do instead of staying at home feeling inadequate with a profound sense of emptiness.

But the complexities of working in the same sport could have been negative, since I was working with the very same players that I was just playing with a year ago. They were playing and I wasn't! But I actually spent those two years in the Orlando front office thinking beyond the position I occupied at the time, thinking about my next transition, fully aware that potentially unforeseen circumstances—such as getting fired—could occur at any time. In hindsight it might have been prudent to take a bit more time to fully experience the trauma of my transition journey. Perhaps finding time to mourn, to complain to anyone who would listen, truly grieve the loss of a career and even do something impulsive were all areas that needed more introspection and time. But in the end those two years allowed me to shake off the cobwebs in my head to get to the next phase.

Since leaving the Magic, I found a variety of things that keep me busy and are fulfilling. I obtained two master's degrees (in sport psychology and in business). I wrote three children's books and two books to help athletes. *Winning the Money Game* addresses managing their finances, and *The Athlete CEO* shows rookies coming into the league how to manage their life and career like the CEO of a corporation. I also released *When the Ball is Laid to Rest*, a book of my poetry that captures the blending of my Caribbean culture with the world of sports. And I continue to run multiple non-profit organizations that satisfy my passions to empower underserved youth and support campaign finance reform in politics.

I have also remained close to the NBA in several ways. I hold basketball camps and give talks to fellow basketball players, serve as Community Ambassador for the Golden State Warriors, I'm a post-game analyst for the ABC affiliate in the Bay Area, and a consultant with the NBA Academy providing life skills to international players. Does this fill the void of not playing for sellout crowds in arenas? Is the money just as good? Of course not. But that's not the point. I have found ways to fulfil my desire to work and contribute during my ongoing transition process.

Immediately after my retirement and for a number of years, I found it extremely difficult to talk about my fears and anxiety about the future with other people. I did view the loss of my career as a death that had to be grieved and mourned. I just didn't think anyone else would understand. Most people think that just because a professional athlete retires with millions of dollars in the bank, he can simply be happy, living off his money for the rest of his life.

Players who are going through similar situations have to understand that they are not alone. Part of their anxiety comes from the fact that they feel like they can't talk about their struggles with anyone. There's an unwillingness to share that type of pain and void. Life after playing in the NBA is a black hole, and nobody really talks about what it looks like because there's a sense of shame in feeling vulnerable. This is especially true for players who were not wise with their money. They are ashamed and don't want anyone to know. And if they are struggling with not knowing what to do next, they may also avoid talking about it because they don't want anyone to think they don't know what they're doing.

But the more you are able to recognize your vulnerability and anxiety, and face your new reality, the more likely you can get through the transition from your athletic career.

Anxiety is defined in a traditional sense as a "feeling of worry, nervousness, or unease, typically about an imminent event or something with an uncertain outcome." In terms of psychiatry anxiety, that is viewed as a "nervous disorder characterized by a state of excessive uneasiness and apprehension, typically with compulsive behavior or panic attacks."

As it pertains to the interviews I conducted, many athletes spoke about their general feelings of worry, nervousness, and uneasiness about retirement; a few even experienced actual panic attacks. However, many spoke about excessive uneasiness, anxiety and apprehension about their retirement future. Others experienced depression, financial hardship, emotional distress, isolation, obesity, gambling and even alcoholism.

Michael Phelps is an American swimmer who is regarded as one of the best swimmer of all time. He holds the record for the most Olympics medals won by any athlete at 28, including 23 gold medals and 13 individual golds. Phelps competed in his first Olympics at the age of 15, as part of the U.S. men's swim team. He was the first American male swimmer to earn a spot on five Olympic teams and also made history as the oldest individual gold medalist in Olympic swimming history at the age of 28.

During the 2016 Summer Olympics in Rio de Janeiro, I remember watching Bob Costas interview Phelps about his first retirement. I was glued to the television. I felt invested in Phelps' journey. He told Costas, "I remember the days locked up in my room, not wanting to talk to anybody, not wanting to see anybody, really not wanting to live. I was on a downward spiral. I was on the express elevator to the bottom floor wherever that might be. And I found it."

When pushed about possibly taking his life Phelps opined, "There were thoughts when I was like, 'How would I do it?' But I knew I never could. Because I knew I would hurt so many people. Me included. The thoughts were there. They were there really heavy. I kind of just started making some progress. I decided something had to change."

Part of the challenge for Michael was that swimming was all he knew. As he puts it, "I only saw myself as a swimmer. That's it. Nothing else. I had no self-worth, no self-love; I was just like, 'Yeah, I'm just a swimmer, I don't have anything else.'"

Former NBA player, Brad Daugherty, arguably one of the best big men in the game, was forced to retire at only 28 years old because of numerous recurring back injuries. His raw unfiltered take on the difficult toll of transition was refreshing and hunting. He warned, "There's no easy transition. I don't care if you play 50 years or have a farewell tour. It doesn't hurt any less. Call it narcissism. Maybe. But it's the damn truth. And it's scary." (*The Transition: Every Athlete's Guide to Life After Sports* / Tennant, Kelli/ 2019)

*Winning the Transition Game*

Here are additional perspectives from other athletes.

**Rashard Mendenhall:** *Career Highlights* Former Pittsburgh Steelers running back who won a Super Bowl in 2009 and amassed a total of 4,236 rushing yards throughout his career.

*Retirement Highlights* At the time of his retirement, he was 26 years old. Eventually, he became a writer and was a writer for the HBO series "Ballers." His transition wasn't a smooth one, however. In fact, he fell into depression before eventually finding prosperity. "When you hear the word *depression*, you think of sadness. Depression, after playing football, was feeling like you don't have a fight, you don't have a cause," he once told a men's magazine reporter. "Who you are, what your purpose is... everything can feel like nothing."

**Darius Miles:** *Career Highlights* At age 18, the former NBA first-round draft pick went from playing at the high school level to immediately earning $3 million in the NBA with the Los Angeles Clippers. He earned $62 million while playing in the NBA but was out of the league by age 27.

*Retirement Highlights* With no college degree or other skillset, Darius eventually filed for bankruptcy in 2016. "My whole life, I used basketball as an escape. When you grow up how I grew up, I think you're probably bound to have some kind of PTSD. I ain't a doctor, but when you grow up running from gunshots all the time, I think there's something inside you that never leaves," he wrote in an essay for The Players Tribune. "I used to feel this *pressure* on me—I'm talking like a physical pressure, you know? But I used to be able to go out onto a basketball court and just unleash it. You could let it all out. Basketball got taken away from me at 27, and I was lost. I was just kind of going through the motions. Then a couple years later, my momma got taken away from me, and I pretty much went insane." Darius continues, "I thought the streets loved me. That was my curse. The streets don't love you like that. The streets don't love nobody. When you're young, you think the money is gonna last forever. I don't care how street smart you are, or who you got in your corner, when you go from not having anything to making millions of dollars at 18, 19 years old, you're not going to be prepared for it."

# PART II:

# CROSSOVER

# Chapter Five

# Phase 4: The Epiphany

*"I know I have always said that there is life after basketball. But all this time, I had wondered if I was going to be ok. My experiences have given me an inkling that I will, in fact, be okay. This might be a beginning of the understanding that there really is life after basketball. There is a place for me in this lost world beyond that of my basketball skills. And, of course, I have always heard that from other people. But this is the first time I really got a first taste of what life after basketball was like. And it did taste good."*

Adonal Foyle, MA, MBA, November 4, 2010,
48 days after retirement

The final phase of the retirement cycle is the epiphany stage. Epiphany has numerous definitions but for the purpose of this book, Webster defines the term as a "sudden manifestation, perception of the essential nature or meaning of something, an intuitive grasp of reality through a simple or striking event, an illuminating discovery, or a realization." That *aha* moment, that hopeful path forward, or the ability to see the light at the end of the tunnel, are all fundamental components of the epiphany stage of the retirement process. This stage is usually viewed as one of the most pivotal stages that can lead to the true beginning of your post-playing life.

## Adonal Foyle, MA, MBA

While I was working on my thesis on retired athletes, for my master's degree in sport psychology at John F. Kennedy University, one of the most common questions people asked me was, "What is the difference between retirement and transition?"

In most lectures at the university, faculty members asserted that an athlete's post-playing experience was a transition. But that didn't sound very convincing to me. I felt that *transition* sounded more like a euphemism of my reality while *retirement* seemed more real and raw to me. I did not want to sugarcoat what I perceived as a perilous path ahead. Part of me didn't really feel like I was transitioning into anything at the level of professional basketball. As someone who had been playing basketball for over 20 years, there was nothing more comforting for me than to be out on the court. If I was transitioning into *something*, in my mind that meant I should be moving into something comparably gratifying to my basketball career. After retiring, I moved into a different aspect of basketball, working as Director of Player Development, but even though I was still in the sport, my new job was nowhere near as exciting as being an actual professional basketball player. I thought that what I was going through could not really be considered a transition. What I did feel was that I had retired and been ripped away from something I loved doing. I did not know what I could "transition" to that could possibly be comparable to that.

NBA players are considered among the top 450 basketball players in the world. It is Ph.D. level. Top Gun level. Navy Seal level. But when a player transitions into another part of his life, he is a rookie all over again. That frightening thought ran through my mind just a couple of months into my retirement.

A player who is starting over is considered a neophyte. A beginner. A novice. He is learning things anew, but most people are already ahead of him. On his first day in the office at his new job, he discovers that everyone else is already leaps and bounds ahead of him. If those same people were to play with him on the basketball court, they would be inept. But now he is the one who is inept! From a psychological standpoint, going from an NBA player to working in an office is like going from a Ph.D. level all the way down to freshman orientation within a one-month span. That scary experience doesn't quite jibe with the whole notion of transition.

With that said, it was clear that I was in a post-playing stage. No matter my next move, I wasn't going to transition into anything comparable to the excitement and satisfaction of being an NBA player. I was no longer part of something that I was pretty darn good at for 20 years. And, whatever my next career was going to be, it was something quite unknown. Obviously, I knew I had the mental capacity to learn something new, but it was still going to take time and a struggle to learn everything I needed to know about how to face this new challenge. I was back to starting at the bottom. So for me, it didn't work when I tried to say that I was in transition. I was a retired professional athlete. Period.

If you're a retired athlete reading this, see if this feeling resonates: "I am shutting down a very large part of my life, which is my active basketball career. And I am trying to transition into something that I am struggling to discover every day. My sport has defined me since I was a teenager. I don't know how this new phase in my life is going to define me. That is what I'm trying to learn in my new world." I will cling to the word "retired" because it's what best described the uncertainty and ambiguity that existed for me at the end of my playing career.

When players walk away from the game, they obviously understand intellectually that they are retired. Emotionally, however, that's a whole other thing. As mentioned earlier, I went straight to the Orlando Magic front office when I retired. Right away, it was clear to me that my emotions were in turmoil every single day. When I would enter the Orlando Magic building, I felt invisible. It was as if my cape that enabled me to accomplish great feats of athleticism was ripped away and discarded. The enormity of the loss manifested itself in large and small ways like missing the thousands of people who were no longer cheering for me; or the forgotten basketball rituals that no longer anchored my routines. I was just expected to do my job. That was my new normal, but it was a struggle to get used to, and I am not sure that I ever really did.

> *Despite my trepidations, there were some bright spots for me after retirement.*

That's not to say people will completely walk away from the allure of even a "former" NBA athlete, and of course superstar athletes are never really forgotten. However, for the most part, retired professional athletes will be jumping into a totally different life that feels much less rewarding, both financially and emotionally.

Despite my trepidations about retirement, there were some bright spots for me after retirement. One of the positive things about being on the other side of the coin was that I was able to think about how I could help other players. As Director of Player Development, I tried to figure out the best way to give them what they needed to be better players. How could I help them to help themselves? One of my greatest assets in this new role was that I was able to put myself in their shoes since I had been there less than a year ago. My new role allowed me to jump in and out of their shoes, to understand and relate to problems they were facing. I could virtually predict how they would respond to certain situations. As a former player, I had a unique perspective which served as a better bridge between the players and the front office. That part was very rewarding for me.

As a member of the front office, I could also learn about the business side of the game that I had always wanted to understand. The more meetings I attended, the greater comprehension I gained of all the different roles needed to manage an NBA team. I always had a good relationship with the general manager of the franchise, but being upstairs now allowed me to see first-hand what his day-to-day operations were like. While I was used to seeing the best athletes perform on the court, I now had an opportunity to see my executive colleagues perform at the highest level in the front office. When I saw that, I realized more and more that there were similarities between what I used to do and what I was now doing. Ultimately, the front office is a group of people doing the best they can to help the team win. I was let go by the Orlando Magic after just two years when almost everyone in the front office was fired at once. But the experience I gained during those two years was extremely valuable.

It was the beginning of my **epiphany**.

Let's look at another epiphany—of someone who was not a professional athlete, but an "average joe" who has been in the trenches of transition and not only learned to embrace the journey, but also came out on the other side better and stronger. Norm Sobel refers to himself as a man of simple tastes, one who finds joy in his life. His is the story of the transition epiphany of a retired furniture manufacturer.

According to Norm, "To fully understand my retirement experience, I think it is important to first talk about the evolution from the beginning. My uncle started the family business in 1939. His two brothers worked for him after they got out of the service. I began to work for the company while I was still in high school, working after school and during summer vacations. At that time, the company manufactured table tops and table bases for restaurants and coffee shops. The San Francisco factory produced table tops and the Los Angeles factory produced the table bases. We started manufacturing booths and banquettes in the Los Angeles factory. When I was 20 years old, I was sent to Hawaii to work in the factory. I was my uncle's eyes and ears, and I ran that operation. I spent one year in Hawaii and returned to the Los Angeles office to work in sales."

But a mere five years later, he was transferred to San Francisco to become the Sales Manager, where he developed substantial relationships with many restaurant owners and interior designers. Eventually, the company was able to expand into hotels, casinos, restaurants and lounges in the gaming industry in Las Vegas. Ultimately, the company would go on to develop hospitals, cafeterias, retirement facilities, and prominent tech companies.

His passion and acceptance of his new reality can be demonstrated by how he approached each day. He gleefully exclaimed that he could not wait to wake up in the morning to go to the office. It was challenging, exciting and very rewarding. He got so much pleasure out of his work but after 55 years, it was time for him to retire.

Norm's retirement came quite as a surprise. He explains:

"My retirement came somewhat suddenly, similar to that of a professional athlete who is called into the office and told that it's time for him to retire. It took a few days for my transition reality to set in. My thought process, because of my makeup, is all positive energy, which is truly important in my life. I do believe that the problem is not really a problem if there is a solution, and I really am blessed to have that philosophy. I looked upon the next part of my life as a wonderful beginning to a new chapter. I do not dwell on negativity; I always accentuate the positive."

After about a year in retirement he reflected about where he was at emotionally, stating that "I have an entirely new daily routine. There are many perks to retirement, flexibility being one of them. Spending time with my four grandchildren, ages three through six is a GIFT. My two wonderful daughters and sons-in-law live in the Bay Area. My wife is my rock! After 45 years of marriage I realize she is the glue that holds it all together. I do believe that any successful relationship is based on two things—a 50/50 split on all decisions and communication. Both are very important to me. This is true with family, friends and team players."

Another important positive impact of his transition is his ability to volunteer for causes he cares about. He expresses his satisfaction, stating "It is so fulfilling to give my time to organizations I strongly believe in. I volunteer at the Jewish Family & Children Services in San Francisco where I call seniors who are a part of the "Safe at Home" program. They are 80 years old and beyond, and often my phone call is their only call of the day. I also consult with the Jewish Vocational Services on a remodeling project at their facility. I will be starting my third volunteer job with the American Cancer Society, 'The Heroes of Hope Program.'"

A third positive effect of retirement for Norm is having the time to read great biographies, a literary genre he adores. He proclaimed, "I am so much more relaxed than I ever thought possible. When I compare my previous work life to my current relaxed life, it is like day and night. I used to work six days a week, 10-12 hour days, taking time off only on Saturdays and evenings. I was a workaholic and loved it. It was my hobby! I believe that if you love what you do for a living, you never have to work a day in your life. I have shared my belief with my daughters, "Have a passion for what you are going to do." I feel so fortunate that my daughters are exceptional at being mothers/wives, and at work."

When Norm reflected on his work-life routine, he said it felt like he was the commander in the control tower at an international airport, except his "planes" were the coming and going of large projects. He talked about being in control from beginning to end, from bidding for the job to completion after manufacturing and the timing of the scheduled shipments. It was a tremendous undertaking, he admitted. He acknowledged that although having those responsibilities was great, not having to deal with them now is even greater.

*This new chapter is so fulfilling because I have time to myself, time with family and friends, and time to do community service.*

With a little smile on his face he exclaimed that this new chapter of his life is so fulfilling because "I have time to myself, time with family and friends, and time to do community service. I do miss some of the business relationships I have made over the many years, particularly in the restaurant field. I have been fortunate that many customers still have businesses in the Bay Area, and I enjoy reconnecting with them when my wife and I dine at their restaurants."

Part of Norm's adjustments in retirement have a great deal to do with his belief in planning ahead wisely. He argues that one must commit to a financial planner at a young age and although it may not seem necessary, he learned it is mandatory. He uses the following example to demonstrate his financial point: At 20 years old, if you save $5.00 a week and put it into a savings account at a modest 1.5% interest rate, 20 years later the face value would be $260.00 per year or $5,200.00 for 20 years. But with compound interest of 1.5%, it would amount to $6,063.00, and if left for 30 years with compounded interest, it would amount to $9,849. He concludes that by the time one turns 50 years old, one can see how much this type of savings would amount to.

The simplicity and pride by which Norm lives his life can serve as an example for many of us. Here are some of the rules he chose to live by:

- What you think of me is not my problem.
- You only get out of something what you put into it.
- Fill your mind and body with positive energy.
- You can think about the negative, but don't dwell on it.
- Common sense is not so common.
- Attitude is a little thing that makes a big difference.
- It is luck that allows common people to obtain uncommon results.
- Take a firm stand to be flexible.

- Be nice to people on your way up because you will meet them on the way down.

- Focus on making things better not bigger.

- The greatest ability is dependability.

The epiphany stage is about crossing over to the stage where you finally think you're going to be okay. It's about having that moment of clarity.

Norm Sobel exemplifies this stage because he has completely embraced his retirement. But it's important to know that no state is permanent, nor is life. Sometimes life is about taking 10 steps forward and 20 steps backwards and you might leapfrog over some stages. Every person is different. Norm's experience can serve as an example of seeing the virtue of every misfortune. His mindset might be his strongest gift of all, for he chooses positivity over negativity.

# Chapter Six

# Shifting your Mindset: Reclaiming the Word "Retire"

*"One doesn't discover new lands without consenting to lose sight of the shore for a very long time."*

**Andre Gide**

One of the things that helped me after my retirement was changing my mindset. My initial mindset regarding retirement was one of fear and anxiety. But later I was able to change that mindset by taking ownership of the word *retire*. I did that by creating an acronym for retire that was more positive than the traditional sense of the word. I have defined that acronym further on.

An athlete's mindset is his mental outlook on life and on his sport. Dr. Carol Dweck makes a distinction between a fixed mindset and a growth mindset in her book *Mindset: The New Psychology of Success*. In it she explains that "In the fixed mindset, everything is about the outcome. If you fail—or if you're not the best—it's all been wasted." In contrast, she argues that the growth mindset "allows people to value what they're doing regardless of the outcome. They're tackling problems, charting new courses, working on important issues."

According to Dweck, "Mindset change is not about picking up a few pointers here and there. It's about seeing things in a new way. When people change to a growth mindset, they change from a judge-and-be-judged framework to a learn-and-help-learn framework. Their commitment is to growth, and growth takes plenty of time, effort, and mutual support."

I had to work hard to change my mindset to one of growth and recommend all players do so in retirement. But for many professional players, a fixed mindset is one of the biggest hurdles for them to get over in their retirement journey.

Mark Blount, a former NBA player, explained the difficulties about the mental side of his transition in the following way:

"For me, the mental side will never go away. It was more about subduing my ego. If someone asked me for advice about how to handle it mentally, I would just tell them to go about it day by day and go from there. Because at one point, we were one of the top basketball players in the world, playing in the best league. A lot of us were lucky to make pensions and do a lot of good things for our families. But the ego is always in us, because we needed it to get us in the league to begin with. That fire is always burning. And that goes back to the patience I was talking about. We always want it and we always want to go get it. It's a mental fight every day. It was bad for me for those first 3-4 years of retirement."

**R.E.T.I.R.E.**

As I have said, the word *retire* conjures up many negative images for professional athletes and others. Retirement feels primarily like loss—loss of social status, loss of identity, loss of relationship, and loss of purpose. By and large most people view retirement as a negative phenomenon because it signifies an ending.

I want to reclaim the word *retire* as positive, to see it as an opportunity to spread our wings and to find new purpose and new meaning in our lives. Each letter of the acronym I created represents a positive element that helped me embrace my retirement.

**Routine**

**Engage**

**Transition**

**Independence**

**Rejuvenate**

**Evolve**

**Routine:**

Part of retirement is a loss of your routine. Routines are one of the essential elements of our work life; therefore, finding routines in your post-career becomes very significant. As a retired person, you need to find a new purpose that includes a routine. One way is to find a hobby that can help you regain your footing. I routinely play racquetball three days a week. Many other activities that can become part of one's routine include joining a book club, planning an annual vacation or staycation, or taking a cooking class.

**Engage:**

One of the problems for many in retirement is managing the desire to retreat into the background or back to your safe place. You may be afraid of facing the world, because of shame due to your circumstances of retirement or fear from the unknown world that awaits you. Isolation becomes a way to deal with retirement. But that isolation and lack of engagement prolong the difficulty of adjusting in a positive way.

Engaging with the world helps you integrate back into society and also helps you to better handle retirement. To engage is to attract attention, get involved, and participate in day-to-day activities with the world. Engagement can take on many forms—making time for your friends, spending time with family, perhaps volunteering, but engaging with others and the world at large.

**Transition:**

I have made my mind up regarding what I perceived as the differences between transition and retirement, but each of you must find the word that work best for you. Transition, like retirement, has a negative connotation. It conjures up fear of what you have lost and fear of where you are going. Transition in and of itself is not a bad thing—it is natural to have some misgivings about retirement or transition, but it's a fear born out of a failure to plan. As an NBA retiree, I had to learn to embrace change by understanding that transition is a process, a time of changing from one state or condition to another that doesn't happen instantaneously. When you think about it, we are transitioning all the time on many different levels: from offense to defense, from one city to another, from life to death, from high school to college, from teenager to adulthood, from single to married or from married to single. We need to treat transition as a natural occurrence. It is true that transition produces a tremendous amount of anxiety. But since transition happens whether or not you want it, the best thing to do is to try to embrace it.

**Independence:**

The whole idea of retirement is that you can finally do the things you want to do with your life. You have spent a tremendous amount of your life working on everything else like having a job, creating opportunities and hopefully saving money for your retirement. Retirement is getting to the point where you can finally grasp that freedom, because you're now attaining a greater sense of independence. Your independence involves doing what you want to do—not what others are telling you to do—spending time with the kids, traveling to a destination you've always wanted to go to, leaving your job, reading those classic books you've always wanted to read, or volunteering for a community service project that you're passionate about. This is your time to truly live for yourself on your own terms.

**Rejuvenate:**

One of the main reasons people retire from professional sports is due to injuries. After years and years of beating up your body, retirement can be a welcome relief, and it becomes an opportunity to rejuvenate your body. Rejuvenation is about making yourself look and feel younger and fresher by giving your body the love and rest it so richly deserves. Imagine a barren flower garden, dry, overgrown with weeds, and picked over by insects. But then you clear the debris, turn over the earth, get rid of the insects, and replant. By doing that, you have put your garden in a position to experience rejuvenation. Similarly, when you retire, you give your body a chance to renew itself.

Imagine finding a blocked creek with fallen trees and branch debris that is preventing the gentle flow of the water. Look at what happens when the debris is removed; the stream flows as it was meant to. Rejuvenation is about reawakening, renewal, and resurgence of all the things your body hopes for in retirement. You can finally take care of your body—engaging in a spa day complete with massage, yoga classes, a meditation session, and a spiritual retreat.

**Evolve:**

The final element of the *R.E.T.I.R.E* acronym is to *evolve*. Evolution is all about who we are as human beings. Look at how many iterations the smartphone we hold in our hands has gone through in just the last several years. As athletes we cannot be afraid of evolving, even if we may at times worry about what we are evolving into. Evolution in its essence is about moving from one phase to the other. If we are not evolving, we are regressing or stagnating. Evolution is an unstoppable force of nature; it cannot be slowed down so we must embrace it. We must! Evolution is the willingness to evolve to the next level, and retirement is all about evolving and growing. If you had stayed stagnant as a player, you would not have progressed very far; you had to constantly improve your basketball acumen and skills development if you wanted to stay on the team. Likewise, in retirement, you must always be evolving, improving your life skills to stay relevant on and off life's bench.

**R.E.T.I.R.E is a Journey, not a Destination**

What some *perceive* to be lost in retirement includes loss of identity, loss of social status, loss of community, loss of financial security, loss of purpose, loss of elite status, loss of baller status, and loss of adoration by fans. Other negative aspects of transition can include depression, weight gain, pain and injuries, and medical concerns. But many others experience positive aspects of retirement, including finding a new vocation, finding a new purpose, spending quality time with family, volunteering in their community, and making time for friendship reconnection.

We must start this journey by reclaiming the word R.E.T.I.R.E. My hope is that reclaiming the word R.E.T.I.R.E. takes away the stigma and the fear that come with the word itself. In the end, no one knows what the final picture will look like, but it is important to understand what others have experienced. Your strongest asset as an individual is the power of your own mindset. Choosing to see retirement as something to conquer, rather than something to fear, can ultimately make all the difference. YOU have the power to choose your path.

In discussing the importance of evolving in transition Dwyane Wade offers this perspective.

"As the world changes, as the world grows, you have to change, you have to evolve, you have to grow." (Dwyane Wade: Inside Heat Star's Last Dance/ Sports Illustrated / by Rohan Nadkarni / 2020)

# Chapter Seven

# Finding your Purpose Again

> *"The mystery of human existence lies not in just staying alive, but in finding something to live for."*
> Fyodor Dostoyevsky, The Brothers Karamazov

Looking back at the many phases of my transition out of the game, it is now clear that the majority of my time was spent finding my footing. Much like a child learning to ride a bike without training wheels, everything I did at first was difficult.

After retiring, you're not sure yet of who you are. I remember going to the weight room for the first time as a former player. I felt awkward on my own with no trainers telling me what to do. But as I got used to it, I got through my workouts more easily. It became easier each time because for the first time in a long time I was working out for me.

*Adonal Foyle, MA, MBA*

I began to understand that no matter how much time you spend as a player—five years, 10 years, 20 years—it is still really only a small part of your entire life. When David Vaughn left the league in 2003, he was 30 years old and unemployed. Whether someone leaves the game at age 40 or 30, or even younger, most of the time that player still has the rest of his life ahead of him.

The good news is that many former professional athletes have been able to find a purpose again for their lives after retirement. J.J. Stokes played nine seasons as a wide receiver in the NFL. He was known mostly as a member of the San Francisco 49ers, but he won a Super Bowl ring with the New England Patriots. Of all the players I interviewed for this project, I found J.J. to be one of the most prepared people for when his playing days were over.

His thought process actually started in college.

"I'd work out during the summer and get ready for the next season. My wife who was my girlfriend at the time would ask me, 'What are you going to do when you're done?'" he told me. "What I did while I was at UCLA was talk to counselors about doing radio work. When I got drafted by the 49ers, I had my agent connect me with a local radio station. At the time, there was just one sports station in the Bay Area so I wanted to do a weekly spot. After the games, I did spots for the sports station in Sacramento. So at the time, I was slowly getting into something I could see myself doing by the time I was done."

J.J. showed a lot of hustle as an NFL player. He did the same off the field. He networked a lot during his career so by the time his career ended, a transition plan was in place. Since he had been doing some radio as an active player, it only made sense for him to go into radio once he was done playing. J.J. did radio shows in the Bay Area as well as in Sacramento. He was also connected to radio personalities in the Modesto area, located in the Central Valley of California. The Modesto station needed a former NFL player to serve as a personality in order to draw in listeners. It was a perfect fit.

J.J. traveled twice a week (a total of six hours on the road) to do a radio show that didn't even pay him. At the time, he didn't care about getting paid. It was a gig he enjoyed doing and he found fulfillment in it. J.J. did the show for two years until an audible came out of nowhere.

"One day, as I'm getting ready to go to work, my partner called to tell me I didn't need to come in anymore. Turns out the housing market had crashed, which meant we lost a lot of advertising revenue and we were no longer on the air. I remember thinking, 'What am I going to do now?'"

With the experience he gained during those two years in radio, along with a number of contacts he made, J.J. went on to his next venture. He devised a plan to return to broadcasting and reached out to his contacts in the Bay Area. He found work doing Internet Radio that reached out to two million listeners nationwide each week. Around the same time, he became part of a TV documentary about his San Francisco 49er teammate, Hall of Famer Jerry Rice. J.J. impressed the producers doing the documentary and they connected him to a TV agent. All of a sudden, J.J. had transitioned from radio to TV. He started off working as an analyst for the Los Angeles affiliate for Fox Sports and, more recently, the Pac-12 Network.

*J.J. Stokes has found much fulfillment and happiness in devoting much of his time to his family.*

He found a way to talk to players about the game he loves. He dipped his hand into coaching for one season with another former NFL player, ex-running back Napoleon Kaufman. The most important transition for him, however, was not necessarily found in a new career. As you will read later on in this book, J.J. found fulfillment and happiness in devoting much of his time to his family.

*Adonal Foyle, MA, MBA*

Because you're reading this book, it may be that you are embarking on your own personal sports retirement journey, and you're wondering what *your* journey will look like. As you read about the journeys of different players I spoke with, you might take comfort, as I did, in seeing what's possible when players like J.J. devise a transition plan as early as college.

Brent Jones, who played with J.J. for the 49ers, also dabbled with TV work immediately after he retired. He did analyst work for CBS, but the grind and demands did not fuel his passion. While talking to Brent, he mentioned one thing that he was always interested in even while he was in the league, and it had nothing to do with sports.

"I started talking to a couple of guys in venture capital whom I met while still playing," Jones said. "When I came back home, I started re-engaging with these guys, who were actually friends. Then I started to think that maybe we could all start our own business. And it's great because the ability to start your own business with a couple of friends brings back the locker room. You all share a passion and everybody works. One day, someone might be the star. Another day, someone else might be the star. Some days, I'm the star because I went out and raised $1 million; as a team, everyone is contributing to the organization. Subsequently, we started our own business. We probably had no business starting a fund, but we didn't know any better because we had an athlete's determination. I was just going to do it. My mentality was, I don't care what people say. I'm going to figure out a way. We obviously had people along the way pointing us toward the appropriate direction."

Brent eventually partnered with former 49ers teammates Mark Harris and Tommy Vardell and started a venture capital firm in 2000. Recently, Brent sold his majority stake in the company.

Earlier in this book, I told the story of my ex-teammate Marc Jackson and his struggles when it came to the boredom of retirement. Despite his initial difficulties, Marc was able to transition successfully.

A Pennsylvania native, he has done analyst work for the Philadelphia 76ers and also keeps himself busy on his ranch when he's not thinking about basketball.

Kristi Yamaguchi continues to stay involved in figure skating by doing analyst work, especially during the Winter Olympics. She continues to write children's books as well as manage her foundation. Meanwhile, Bret Hedican is still doing analyst work for the NHL and started another business in 2014, a sports team management startup in Vancouver.

Along with his continued work with me during my basketball camps, Roy "Zazu" Byrd also found passion outside of his sport with cigars. He currently has his own business and is often called upon to host cigar parties for other professional athletes and high-level executives around the Bay Area. "It's energizing learning about the cigar industry and building relationships with the manufacturers, owners and other cigar experts," Roy told me. "It's like another brotherhood that I'm forming that's beyond basketball. You can get a lot of deals done while smoking cigars. It's just like sipping wine. I'm now in a totally different world. It's a smoky world, but it's an awesome world. It has its ups and its downs; you have your cigar snobs, you have wannabe smokers, and you have guys who smoke $40 cigars and look down on people who can only afford $5 cigars. But it's not about the price—it's about the experience. And that's what people get confused about."

David Vaughn is also back on his feet. "I work for the state of Florida in the department of children and family services in Orlando. I work with the food stamps, cash and Medicaid programs as an intake specialist for their economics program. I work a 40-hour week. I answer a lot of phone calls. I hear a lot of complaints. I hear a lot of people wanting their benefits right then and there, and I have to explain to them that it doesn't work that way. There's a process. But I deal with it. It's a good job for me. I'm thankful to even have a job. I had to go through two months of training. And I actually earned the right to be there because I passed all the exams."

> *The point of developing a transition game plan for your retirement is to pursue and unlock a new passion that will give you purpose for the rest of your life.*

It is important to understand that no matter what you do, whether it's working for the state or running your own business, it will not deliver the euphoria that came with performing at the highest level in front of screaming fans. But the point of developing a transition game plan for your retirement is to pursue and unlock a new passion that will give you purpose for the rest of your life.

Many professional athletes have had very successful retirements. They have made successful transitions into refereeing, coaching, business, academia, finance, general manager, media, movies, charity, elite basketball training, real estate, franchising, and even international basketball. Athletes who went from playing professional basketball to refereeing in the NBA include Bernie Fryer, Leon Wood, and Haywoode Workman. Similarly in the NFL there are several retired athletes turned NFL officials including Nate Jones, Terry Killens, Dave Hawkshaw, Jimmy Russell, Patrick Holt, and Tripp Sutter.

National basketball and football commentators include Michael Strahan, Howie Long, Troy Aikman, Jenifer Azzi and Chris Mullin, Reggie Miller, Chris Webber, Charles Barkley, Jalen Rose, and Kenny Smith, not to mention the number of such retired athletes at the collegiate level. There are many who made it in franchising like George Tinsley and Junior Bridgeman.

In the realm of coaching we've seen the success of people like Steve Kerr, Derek Fisher, Jason Kidd, Isaiah Thomas, Lenny Wilkins, and Brian Shaw. Finally there is the success of business ventures like Big3 and the numerous NBA players involved in that venture, and the successes of business moguls such as Magic Johnson, Shaquille O'Neal and Michael Jordan.

These success stories are a lighthouse in the distance beckoning us to the possibilities of what could be. In times of uncertainty and fear, we can look to those stories for motivation.

It pays to remember, as athletes, what stock you came from and that in the journey ahead you will find hidden gems and resources within you. Athletes are a force of nature with an incredible inventory of gifts.

Think of the powerful characteristics that are common amongst elite athletes including qualities such as competitiveness, commitment, focus, drive, discipline, self-confidence, aggressiveness, raw talent, determination, adaptability, emotional maturity, natural leadership, teamwork, and passion.

As athletes you accept that mistakes are part of the game, you don't dwell on the past, you possess a high tolerance for pain, you have a unique ability to manage stress, you have a special ability for resilience, and you are able to learn from setbacks.

These amazing qualities are still within you. But you must learn to align them to a different purpose. That purpose is to learn how to create a meaningful life after retirement.

Every person I've mentioned in this book credits the help of others for getting them where they are. You are not alone. You need people.

The road ahead for many retired athletes is a multifaceted rainbow of opportunities which requires one to dawn a new cape or wear a different hat. Many retired athletes pursue unique adventures way outside the gaze of their former profession. Former NBA player Shandon Anderson is now working as a chef at a vegetarian restaurant, former NBA player Chris Dudley now a politician, former NBA player Vinnie Johnson has gone into business in the field of manufacturing, former 16 year NBA player Detlef Schrempf launched a venture capital firm, and Mark Blount's entrepreneurial passion is real estate. Michael Jordan is a team owner, Grant Hill an African American art collector, former NBA player Etan Thomas an author, motivational speaker, and host of *The Rematch*, Roy Byrd a cigar business owner, Kobe Bryant an Oscar winner, Marc Jackson a horse ranch owner, Bryant Reeves became a cattle rancher, Kristi Yamaguchi an author and fashion designer for her own clothing line, and former major league pitcher Randy Johnson is now a photographer.

> **Dwyane Wade Career Highlights**: a 16-year NBA playing career, highlighted by three NBA Championships, 13-time All-Star.
>
> **Retirement Highlights:** In a recent conversation with *Sport Illustrated* during his number retirement, he talked about his perception and reality of retirement. "You know what? I actually thought I was going to miss the game more than I have so far. I had a quick moment when I decided to retire that I got nervous. I got nervous about letting something go that I've been doing my entire life. And I've been good at it for a long time. But immediately, I feel I'm so blessed to put myself in the position and to be put in the position where I have people around me that are go getters. We hit the ground running right away to like, we need to get the next phase going now. I've been able to keep myself and my mind busy and put it into something else. I've really been focused on building what's to come."

In talking about how he views transition a few months beyond the game and after the death of Kobe Bryant, Dwayne Wade spoke of the weight of the legacy he must carry on. "I feel even more responsibility now than I did a month ago, because Kobe was leading this charge. Kobe was the leader of the new generation. " Wade added that Michael Jordan "showed us that you could continue a legacy through sneakers. Magic showed us you can build a business through so many different outlets. Kobe was showing us that you could create stories and win an Oscar. I'm focused on being that leader Kobe was for me and for others. To show the athletes that's coming up this is how you do it differently. Retirement is not the end of your life. Retirement is the end of a chapter, but you can do these amazing things in the next chapter." (Nadkarni, 2020)

The vision and the responsibility laid out by Wade is quite promising for the future of our sport. In a world where transition is viewed as a negative phenomenon, his perspective can be a game changer. Dwayne Wade may have indeed stumbled onto his purpose.

# PART III:

# Winning the Transition Game

# Chapter Eight

# 21 Ways to Win The Transition Game

> *"My initial 60 days, which consisted of me getting my master's degree, was good because I spent time interviewing nine ex-players. And that was very therapeutic because I had a foreshadowing of what I would go through. In a way, that helped me; it wasn't as foreign to me as I once thought. Although I know it didn't make things easier, it did make it easier than if I didn't have them. This was an amazing journey of self-discovery and something athletes can learn from."*
>
> **Adonal Foyle, MA, MBA Journal Entry: February 23, 2011**
> **Six months after retirement**

As I am putting this book together, the stark truth is that I'm still in the middle of my transition. I haven't suited up for a game in over 10 years. Since my retirement, I've become a writer, TV/radio analyst, motivational speaker and philanthropist, and much like the dilemmas that Bret Hedican revealed, there is the temptation to do too much. There's nothing necessarily wrong with that, as the point of this book is to get players to think about what's next in their career after sports. Discovery and experimentation are very much a part of the journey. It's one thing to have too many things going on—it's quite another to have no plan at all.

Throughout this book, you've learned about the difficulties that can result when a detailed transition plan is not in place, and you've read about those who continued to struggle even when they had resources at their disposal. If you're a professional athlete reading this book, I will ask the same question my dad asked me: What are you going to do?

**1) Take Your Time... and Hurry Up**

Circumstances will dictate the next phase. If you have a lot of money, you can take a little more time to think of what you want to do next. If you have hobbies, you may be able to distract yourself before choosing whether or not one of those hobbies becomes your next career. Whatever you do, it will initially be *just* a hobby. But there will come a time when you will start asking yourself if you want to turn that hobby into a career.

**2) Start Planning Now**

My cousin and former international basketball player, Alexus Foyle, when asked about what he thought about retirement, honestly admitted, "To tell you the truth, I thought I was going to play basketball forever. I never thought I would have to retire. I knew in the back of my mind I would at some point because of Father Time, but I really did think I would be playing forever."

In contrast to Alexus' experiences, J.J. Stokes began his plan as early as college by networking with people within the radio sector. The point is, he began networking as soon as he started connecting with people in different industries. It may have come easy for J.J. at the time, as he was a breakout wide receiver at UCLA and was on the verge of becoming a first-round draft pick.

*If you're serious about staying in sports in a different capacity, you must be able to put in the work.*

It's natural for athletes to think about staying in sports once they're done playing, but jobs in the field of sports are few and far between. Not only are you competing with other former athletes who are trying to find their way during their post-playing career, you are also competing with seasoned veterans who have been in the industry for years, if not decades. So if you're serious about staying in sports in a different capacity, you must be able to put in the work to start creating your transition playbook.

### 3) Network, Network, Network

About a month prior to the 2018 NBA Draft, former NBA player Damon Stoudemire posted the following tweet to his followers:

"Any youngster advisor, family member of a potential draftee. Holla at me. Ask me questions. No need to bump ya head when people before u can help. Free of charge. Quit making a simple process hard. Protect the youth. They are the future."

In effect Damon was asking future stars to not make the mistake of past players but instead reach out to those former players for advice and mentorship.

Hundreds of questions were asked; most of them received a response. But there was one question that I was most interested in:

"What is your best advice for recently retired players struggling to transition into a second career?"

Almost immediately, Damon provided this response: "Relationships," he tweeted. "If you didn't nurture them while you played it will be hard while you're out. Hopefully you can make decisions not based on money. Lastly, set your ego to the side. Goes a long way."

*Adonal Foyle, MA, MBA*

As long as you're an active player in the league, you are considered a one-man institution. This means you have unbelievable access to people and places you wouldn't have if you weren't a player. If you're interested in a certain industry, contact a company CEO and let them know that you are interested in knowing more about a career in that industry and the company. We are now hearing more and more about pro athletes spending the off-season serving as interns at tech companies, or doing fellowships at hospitals, or even working on their craft in front of a TV camera. You just have to take the first step and be willing to say that you would like to learn something new.

Being an active player in the league also means leveraging your resources and inviting business leaders to a game. So many players are used to being approached by fans and business people who are either looking for autographs or selfies, that players mindlessly oblige. What they don't do is engage with these business people and get to know them and their companies.

Players who are still active in the league have the ultimate power in getting great seats for VIPs. The players are already serving the community with team functions but it's crucial to take it a step further and invest time in knowing more about business and its leaders. NBA players have the best advantage when it comes to this because they can actually engage with them during games. In the NFL, players are hidden behind their helmets and they have a tough time engaging with their invited guests, most likely because they are sitting in a suite above the stadium. Baseball players may be able to invite guests to sit behind home plate, but there's usually not much interaction since the player is either in the dugout or on the field. And hockey players can't interact with fans due to a thick piece of plexiglass between them. For as long as you are active in the league, you have access to anyone at any time you want. You'd be surprised how many players don't see it that way.

While I was interviewing Brent Jones for this book, he realized just how much he missed out on networking because of the simple fact that he was playing a different sport.

# Winning the Transition Game

 *It's all about leveraging your relational capital.*

"In the NBA, it's so easy," Brent said. "You walk around and shake hands with the people who are sitting courtside. A couple of years ago, I had courtside seats because my buddy was a top venture guy, and another guy was a top CEO. You're sitting next to these guys and the players don't even try to talk to them. I'm like, 'Dude, you can be set for life.' These guys sitting courtside can help you understand the business world. And I get it, players need that focus for the game, but after the game or before the game, why not talk to the business people? We know how expensive those seats are. It's like a lay-up. In football, we don't have that. We can't walk up to the most expensive luxury box and start shaking hands after the game. It's about building relationships while you still have something special, while you still have the job title. It's all about leveraging your relational capital. Whether it's working with some business guy's young son on some basketball moves, or bringing them to a game. Little things like going out of your way and meeting new people who are typically not on your radar as a current player."

## 4) Do Your Homework

Regardless of what field you want to get into, and no matter how many contacts you're able to make, it's still on you to do the necessary research about the career you're interested in. The important thing to remember is that when you find what you want to do, you will likely start back at the bottom of the totem pole, so be willing to start over and learn. After all, you started playing basketball knowing nothing too.

 *It's imperative to do whatever it takes to gain a necessary edge.*

And yes, this starting-over applies to superstar players. If you won multiple championships, but you suck in front of a camera, you're not going to be given that TV analyst gig. So the next thing you'll need to think about is how you are going to compete with those who have been in the business for 20-30 years. That's not an easy thing.

It's imperative to do whatever it takes to gain a necessary edge. Think of it as being back in competition. You're going to do all you can to win that job over someone else. If it means a few extra hours hitting the books, then so be it.

Also, keep in mind that, depending on what sport you're in, the four major sports leagues have resources that can help you when it comes to selecting your second career. Some leagues are more proactive than others, but they can help you nonetheless. The National Basketball Retired Players Association, for example, partners with Syracuse University's communications department and has a joint program that helps players go back to school and train for on-air media opportunities.

**5) Don't Find Your Next Job. Find Your Next Career.**

If you are one of those athletes who was able to manage your money well, then you can view your transition time as an opportunity to search for something you truly love to do. In other words, don't find a job right away for the sake of finding another job. If at all possible, you should take your time because you want to know and prepare for what the next challenge is going to be. You might not find your "perfect" job right away, but it's always good to keep asking yourself, "What are my interests? What are my passions?" You might not be able to answer those questions immediately upon retiring from sports but whatever you do, don't look for a "job." Look for something you always wanted to do, whether it's a hobby or other interest. Life can get miserable very fast if you simply find a job for the sake of having a job.

**6) Transition is Necessary**

Transition is necessary for the professional athlete because it is a call to action after suffering the loss of a career as an active player. It doesn't matter how much money you have in the bank. Think of it this way; even if you're a billionaire and someone you love passes on, you are going to be in pain. Even if you have a lot of money saved up and you can no longer play the game that you have been playing as a child, in high school, in college, and as a pro, you are going to be in pain because you've suffered a loss. Loss is universal. We all experience it, and we all grieve from it. My dad used to always say to me, "We are all born with a terminal disease—death." It's the one universal thing we all share no matter the circumstances in society.

I believe the terminal disease of death, the loss, the grieving, also holds true in a career. If you are passionate about something, and you spend your entire life pursuing that passion as your career, and all of a sudden, you can no longer do it, the loss is very real. I'm telling you that it's okay to grieve your loss and talk about it with others.

As I've already said earlier in the book, transition is not something to figure out *when* you're transitioning. You must think about it during the course of your career, simply due to the *nature* of your career (you may play for up to 15 years, but that's still a very small part of your life). A doctor can theoretically practice medicine until the day he dies. Even golfers can play for far longer than football, basketball or baseball players. Any players in the four major sports can spend up to 15 years being the best at what they do. But when that's taken away from them, they virtually have to start all over again.

## 7) Sign up with your union

When athletes retire, they tend to disappear without leaving an address where people can find them. Most professional sports have a union for former athletes. It is important to join the retired players associations to ensure you have access to their services. For example, the National Basketball Retired Players Association (NBRPA) is a non-profit organization that is supported by the NBA and National Basketball Players Association (NBPA). The NBRPA mission is to assist former NBA, ABA, Harlem Globetrotters and WNBA players with their transition away from their careers as professional athletes. In addition, the NBRPA works to positively impact communities and youth through basketball and mentorship.

Similarly, according to its mission statement posted on the website, the Retired Football Players Association (RFPA) is "dedicated to providing powerful national advocacy and collegial support for retired professional football players, their families and the community at large. The RFPA's specific area of focus is to raise awareness and funding in support of medical research in the areas of Alzheimer's and ALS, particularly as it relates to repeated head trauma. The RFPA provides financial assistance for members suffering from these illnesses. Additionally, the RFPA lobbies nationally for more comprehensive medical benefits for retired athletes."

These institutions can be holding licensing money for players. They take care of your pension and many are offering cheaper health care for retired athletes along with other services.

## 8) Financial Stress Test

As you approach retirement, it is important that you and your financial team prepare a financial stress test which involves assessing your financial realities, including tax liability, portfolio performance and living expenses. The financial stress test is about doing a financial

MRI to assess your capabilities and see how your finances are going to perform when you retire. These decisions could inform what job you take, where you live, how many people you can support and whether or not you have the financial means to have a healthy successful retirement.

**9) Health Screening**

In retirement, with the loss of the vigorous schedule and training, players can become susceptible to serious medical issues. A recent report claimed that since 2000, more than 50 former NBA players have died of complications related to heart disease (*BillyPenn.com*). When players walk away from the game, they can become unhealthy, gain weight, or have medical issues that were not sufficiently diagnosed and may cause problems in retirement. Therefore it is very important that every player undergoes health screening for everything, from prostate cancer to heart disease to their overall health. It's like a stress test for your body in your post-career.

Under the leadership of Michele Roberts, the National Basketball Players Association enlisted the help of the Athletic Heart Institute to provide free heart screening services for current and former NBA Players. This outreach effort has become a life-saving endeavor in early detection of heart conditions that can pose serious health risks to Athletes.

**10) Mental Health Check**

Mental health continues to be viewed in the sporting world as something to hide—like a volcano boiling right beneath the surface waiting to explode. Kevin Love, an NBA player with the Cleveland Cavaliers penned an article in *The Players Tribune* entitled "Everyone is Going Through Something," where he spoke candidly about a panic attack that occurred during a game against the Atlantic Hawks. Love described his panic attack in excruciating details:

"After halftime, it all hit the fan. Coach Lue called a timeout in the third quarter. When I got to the bench, I felt my heart racing faster than usual. Then I was having trouble catching my breath. It's hard to describe, but everything was spinning, like my brain was trying to climb out of my head. The air felt thick and heavy. My mouth was like chalk. I remember our assistant coach yelling something about a defensive set. I nodded, but I didn't hear much of what he said. By that point, I was freaking out. When I got up to walk out of the huddle, I knew I couldn't reenter the game—like, literally couldn't do it physically".

This brave act by Kevin Love ignited a conversation about mental health that moved the NBA and other professional teams to act and take decisive action to help athletes. This conversation clearly affected retired athletes as well some of whom are dealing with some mental challenges of thier own. As we have seen in this book, transition can be a combination of both positive and negative experiences. To help unravel some of the challenges that can potentially plague professional athletes it can be very useful to find a mental health professional who will help walk you through some of the obstacles and some of the blockages in your thinking. A mental health professional can help you find your way through your transition by providing an outlet who will listen and challenge you when necessary. A therapist can also help give you the right footing for your retirement journey.

## 11) Volunteer

It is important for athletes to feel valuable, and one of the ways to do that is to be of service to others. Athletes still have a lot of political cachet, and going out and helping in your community will not only give you a sense of purpose, but a sense of doing something good for others. Volunteering in your community is about showing the world the positive difference you are making in the lives of others.

## 12) Re-education

Many professional athletes leave college early without a degree. Re-education is about taking an assessment of your academic records and seeing how close you might be to completing your degree. This assessment is about preparing yourself for the road ahead. It might be even possible to return to your college and complete your degree. I was able to finish my degree at Colgate while I was still in the NBA. I also started a master's degree in sport psychology, and when my career was over I went back and earned an MBA with the help and resources of the National Basketball Retired Players Association. Many athletes have to figure out where the gaps in their academic environment exist, and how to close those gaps in order to be more marketable.

## 13) Share your stories with others

By virtue of being former professional athletes, players have amazing stories to tell about resilience, overcoming obstacles, beating the odds, and being the best in their field. These stories are powerful and they can help the next generation find their footing and their courage. Willingness to share these stories with the world can really help other people and empower future athletes. These stories can be useful to corporations by giving them ways to motivate their employees.

## 14) Research your family history

Athletes have the time in retirement to reconnect with their families and friends. Trying to connect with your family tree can give you a sense of your own history. Unearthing your cultural background and where you came from can help you develop a strong sense of who you really are. Researching your family's history can reveal a lot about how you have certain tastes or act a certain way. It can also help establish your authentic core identity as well as see ancestral patterns of overcoming failures and surviving hard times. Knowing your family history can give you a lot of power in knowing that you are not alone. Sites like Ancestry.com and 23andMe are great ways to track your history.

**15) Mentor**

Young people are eager for a sense of direction and professional athletes can help fill that void. How amazing it can be to have a professional athlete showing you the ropes about what it takes to be a good athlete. Retired pro athletes have so much to share by becoming a big brother to a young aspiring athlete. By becoming a mentor to somebody else, and sharing your knowledge with them, they can empower the next generation to find their purpose. There are numerous benefits to becoming a mentor which include the importance of staying relevant. A second benefit of becoming a mentor involves teaching which reinforces your own skills. Other benefits of mentorship include cultivating your network of peers, increasing your leadership and management abilities, and improving our overall athletic industry.

**16) Reflection Journal**

During my first hundred days of transition, I kept a journal called *100 days of transition*. It was a powerful tool that helped me to be mindful of what I was thinking and to recognize what I was feeling. Journaling gives you a tremendous perspective about what you are going through and what you are experiencing. You are able to reflect on your journey, to be aware of all of the experiences you are going through. Journaling was one of the most fruitful experiences that I engaged in and it has enabled me to write this book about my transition.

## 17) Focus on the positive aspects

There is a tendency when you go into a difficult situation to focus only on the negative aspect of your experience. It is important for athletes and people going through transition in general to not only recognize the negative but also to focus more on the positive. By focusing on the positive you will see that your experience is no different than many others. Transition doesn't only have to look at what you lost. You should identify what you've gained. The opportunity to experience something new in the future can be amazing and can be very helpful with your transition.

## 18) Maintain your sense of humor

It is so important when you go through a difficult period not to lose perspective, but, more importantly, not to lose your sense of humor. The ability to laugh at yourself is a useful skill and a vital part of dealing with adversity. The ability to laugh even when things are going badly is a useful skill. Remembering to laugh and smile are the things that can bring you a little bit of sanity in your life, especially when things are chaotic.

## 19) Find a role model

It is important for an athlete to find a role model that can inspire and motivate them through their transition process. You're not the first and you're not going to be the last to go through retirement. It is important to go out and search and find somebody who can help you to cross over into transition. Stories and lessons learned from people who've been through the very same thing that you're going through can be powerful. As an athlete you might want to start a business where former players are already in that very business who can provide meaningful resources, best practices and pitfalls to avoid.

Call them and ask them to be a resource. They may be able to help you avoid making the same mistakes that they've already made in the past. For example, LeBron got input from Warren Buffet.

**20) Relying on Faith**

Many athletes use their faith to help them deal with thier transition. When asked about how she coped with that feeling of loss once she was no longer a basketball player, Ruthie Bolton relied on her faith to get through those difficult days of no longer playing in the WNBA.

According to Ruthie: "That's when my faith stepped in. And all I could think was 'Whatever God gave me, nobody could take that from me.' I remember getting into a car accident in 1985. I was thrown out of my car after being hit by an 18-wheeler. I didn't have my seatbelt on. My family found me laying in a ditch. And when they found me, my head was laying on a Bible. People see that as a coincidence. But for me, I felt like God was preparing me for the rest of my life. I had a lot more work to do. I still had a lot of struggles to go through. I still had a lot of mountains to climb. When I was cut by the Sacramento Monarchs, that was a really hard blow for me. I wanted to have hate. I wanted to have resentment. But I had to aim higher than that. And that's why I created my nonprofit 'Aim High.' Yes, I was frustrated. Yes, I gave so much to my team. But my dad told me to never let anyone take away my power. That's easier said than done, but creating Aim High helps me help others deal with anger, having a different mindset and a different attitude, choices, habits, accountability and overcoming adversity. How to aim higher. So through my adversity, I found out who I really was."

**21) Set up a transition game plan**

As athletes we are used to having a playbook filled with plays. Your transition playbook is your road map to your transition. NBA players and teams can have over one hundred defenses/offenses sets in their playbook. All of the elements we have outlined in this book are important parts of your transition playbook. Start planning and working on your transition playbook including all the things you want to do when you transition out of the sprots realm. Some of the elements should include looking at your financial plan, looking at your mental health plan, looking at your medical plan, looking at your family plan, and looking at your living arrangements. All of these things become a part of your transition playbook.

I urge you: Start brainstorming and planning today.

**10 questions to ask yourself during your athletic transition (for those who don't know where to start):**

1. Did you get out of the house today?
2. Did you read a book?
3. Did you call a friend?
4. Did you talk to someone about the pain?
5. Did you write down all your hobbies?
6. What career did you think about doing before becoming a basketball player?
7. What was your favorite subject in school?
8. Did you take a Myers-Briggs Personality Assessment Test to show what field you may be interested in?
9. Did you call your university about finishing your degree?
10. Did you call your former team to investigate what opportunities for employment might be available for you?

# Chapter Nine

# Transition Stories from the Trenches

### (From Former Pro Athletes, Civilian Personnel and Military Personnel)

> *"A lot of people resist transition and therefore never allow themselves to enjoy who they are. Embrace the change, no matter what it is; once you do, you can learn about the new world you're in and take advantage of it."*
>
> **Nikki Giovanni**

As an athlete, you've been programmed. Part of your DNA is to compete every day, whether it's in your sport, or good investment opportunities, or the best deal on a car. You're always in the mix, you're always trying to accomplish something, and you're always trying to win. The hardest part when you're cut loose, whether you retire or are forced out because of injury, is you don't know where to compete. That's the number one concern. The other significant issue is what I call the locker room effect. You always had a support system, whether it was club ball, in high school, in college, or in the pros. In all of those levels, there's a locker room. You have relationships, you have support. Kind of like a safety net.

In the locker room, you have management and other people looking out for you. There are people there to get you to the right place at the right time. Guys you can talk to about basic and mindless things. The minute you're out, you lose that. You still have your friends, but all of a sudden you're not going through the same experience; they continue their daily practice and conditioning routines while you're now on the outside looking in.

Trying to figure out *where* your locker room is after your career is over is a huge thing. Going solo doesn't work for anybody.

I interviewed the following people to collect their thoughts and personal action plans on their transition after their illustrious careers. As you read what they have to say, think of how you can apply the lessons they learned to your own retirement journey.

*Winning the Transition Game*

**Juan Carlos Gomez**

Retired, US Marine Corp
Active 1997-2003

*When did you enter the military?*

I joined the military in 1997. I was 18 at the time.

*Talk about your experience in the military.*

I served nine years in the Marine Corps. When you sign up for the military, you come away either loving it or hating it. And I loved the Marine Corps. Even though it had its ups and downs like anything else, I loved it because of the friendships and camaraderie.

Throughout my career, I went from unit to unit to unit (similar to when a professional athlete goes from team to team to team). Every time you change units, you move to different environments and create new friendships. You get used to that. It's a lifestyle. I might have made more money doing something else, but I wouldn't have had that close, tight-knit group that I was so tight with. That's what you miss when you're no longer in the military.

*What was the first year like when you came home? What challenges did you experience?*

One of the main stressors I had was not knowing what I wanted to do next. It's different than when you're 18 and graduating high school. Now I was in my 30s so I knew I needed to have a plan.

In the military, you are so controlled. They control when you eat, when you go to sleep, this, that and the other. It's like you're a freaking machine. Once you don't have that, you have to man up and make your own decisions. So that added a bit of stress to my transition. At the same time, I was focused more. I was like, "Okay, let me put my pieces together, step by step." You can't do it all at once. But once you start getting on track and go from being a soldier to a civilian, it becomes second nature. You just have to adapt.

**When did you finally figure out what you wanted to do?**

My girlfriend actually convinced me to get into finance because she had been in finance forever. So I thought, why not give it a shot, and I ended up getting my degree in finance, and she helped me get a financial job in New York City. Like I said, you go through experiences. And when I first got out, I had some experiences. I worked at other jobs and I hated them. Because another thing you encounter is that you're used to a certain lifestyle.

Just like in the NBA, there are guys who love what they do; they travel all the time, and when you're done, you miss the traveling, you miss the action, the love of the game. I had a love for what I did in the military. You don't have a 9-to-5 in the military—it's a 24/7 job and every day is different. Then you go from that to a job from 8:30 am to 7 pm and I found out quickly that that was not for me. I needed to do something I love.

So after thinking long and hard, and with my girlfriend supporting me all the while, I started thinking, what about cigars? After my girlfriend and I started getting more serious, we bought a condo in New Jersey and I ended up in a cigar shop. I met a great guy, Willie, who eventually became my partner. And Willie's partner in the business was someone I had known since I was 12 years old. Small world. One thing led to another and I ended up learning about and working on the retail side of cigars. Willie used to be a wholesaler so one day the thought came to me, why can't we do both? So here I am, with a cigar company that we re-launched under Willie's old brand in 2011. The brand is called Lahoa; it means "Leaf."

*Winning the Transition Game*

When it came to my transition, I had a plan, but it changed. One thing I found out: you just don't get out of the military without a plan.

**Talk about the relationships you made in the military. How have those relationships continued or changed?**

There are a handful of people that I still talk to. Those are the ones I consider true brothers. Being a kid, I was told by people like my father that if I join the Marine Corps, I'll be a man. I believe I was a man before I even joined and that was because of my father. He taught me a lot. I'm a strong believer that when it comes to friends, I'd rather have four quarters than a hundred pennies. In the military, I got close with a small group of friends who I still talk to every day. We're involved in each other's lives even if we live far away.

**What were your thoughts on leaving the military before you actually got out?**

One thing's for sure. It completely changed my life in terms of how I acted every day. When you're 18 and leaving high school, and you're used to Mom and Dad waking you up and making your bed in the morning, you're in a completely different situation than when you're in the military. They crack the whip and you learn that very quickly, especially during boot camp.

I liked the military from the first day I arrived. I think for some people it's harder to adapt because they're not used to authority, but for me, I was used to it. Although I knew I could use the military as a retirement tool, unfortunately for me, through my process of going through retirement, the war broke out. So that chapter in my life really weighed heavily as to why I got out.

War leaves a scar on you that a lot of people don't understand even if you explain it. It's very deep. At the time, I had a daughter. She's 14 now. I decided, not only for myself, but for her. If I had gone back, I probably wouldn't be here.

*Adonal Foyle, MA, MBA*

*How many friends did you lose along the way, and how does that play in your soul?*

It's tough. In our unit, we lost quite a few people. People I interacted with, and maybe two close friends, which still hurts. Then you start to feel guilty that you struggle to overcome. And you start to think about what could have been done differently in that situation. But I understand now that nothing different could have been done. If it's meant to be, it's meant to be... you have to move on with life. That's very hard for a lot of Marine Corps servicemen; moving on. It's really tough. A lot of people have to go to therapy. A lot of people, especially those who went into combat, are dealing with PTSD. I never thought much about PTSD but it's a real problem because you go through certain emotions and when you're outside of the military, you still feel a lot of the weight of what happened.

*When you have a normal day, and your mind goes back to those friends, how does that affect you? Does it stop you in your tracks or do you become contemplative about it?*

Now, it makes me appreciate life more. Whereas before, it was sadness and guilt. Now that I'm much older, I can carry on. Life is precious.

*What was that feeling like, coming home and being back in your daughter's life?*

My situation was a bit different. While I was in the Marine Corps, I was married for five years. We ended up being divorced because Marine Corps life is very tough because I was away for months on end, and as a result, we grew apart. When I did leave the Marine Corps, I made a decision that the only way I was going to be focused is if I came home to where my family was; they really helped me a lot.

My family is from New Jersey, not California so I had to decide to leave my daughter and when I moved across the country, I was already out of the military. I focused, got my degree, and now I'm in the cigar business, which is my lifeline. If I hadn't done that, perhaps I wouldn't be where I am now. And what good am I to my daughter if I can't support her? She's a beautiful, happy 14-year-old; she comes to visit me twice a year. She loves New York. I feel like now I'm able to be a good parent.

**When I talk to people coming out of the military, one of the things they say is that it's difficult to ask for help. Why did asking for help come so naturally to you?**

Fresh out of the military and fresh out of combat, you can turn to friends but they can only do so much for you. Because a lot of my friends have been through the same thing, we know that we all need help. I'm not a big person to see a shrink or therapist, but I did see a few. They helped a little bit, but I think the core of help came from, and continues to come from, my family. And that's why family is very important.

**A soldier calls you to tell you he's thinking about leaving the military. What would you tell him to expect?**

First, I'm going to ask him why he wants to leave the military, and if he's sure. The grass isn't always greener on the other side. In the military, you have a salary, you have a job that you really can't get fired from (unless you do something really bad). Why would you leave?

If he still wants to leave, I would tell him to expect challenge after challenge after challenge. Because not only is he going to encounter the challenges of finding a job and making money, he's also going to encounter people who will love him for his service, and people who will hate him. He will have to learn to balance both. It will be essential that he's mentally ready. Then again, you have to be mentally ready for anything in life. You have to be mentally prepared. Mentally strong. And if you hit a roadblock, you get back on the road. You don't stay down.

*Adonal Foyle, MA, MBA*

*What three things have helped you the most with your transition?*

First and foremost, prayer. I have a strong relationship with God that runs very deep. Prayer with God has helped me a lot, emotionally. Second, family. Blood is thicker than water; having a good father and mother to go to... to talk to... to cry with... to get support from; anything helps. Third, I would say close friends. Real close friends will back you up. They won't give you bogus, meaningless answers. They will say things to you that you don't want to hear and that's very important during transition.

You mentioned the possibility of a soldier coming home to people who hate you. What has your experience been like?

Although there wasn't any name calling, it was more like, "You went out there and killed innocent people. This government is wrong." Everyone has their own opinion but at the end of the day, be glad you're in a country where you're free to give your opinion, and not be arrested for it. That's what we fight for.

*What role did the military play in your transition, if any?*

The military experience alone gives you a lot of tools that you can use throughout life like discipline, accountability, and strategic thinking, so I was able to utilize some of the tools I learned.

*What does the future look like for you?*

I think the future is very bright. None of us can predict the future but the way I put my pieces together, I'm starting to see a picture.

*Speak to your 18-year-old self who is about to join the military. What would you say to him?*

I would just tell him to stay focused. Life is going to throw you anything and everything possible to stop you in your tracks. But even if you feel like you're out for the count, keep pushing. Get up.

*Adonal Foyle, MA, MBA*

## Brent Jones
**Retired, NFL Tight End**
**Active 1987-1997**

*Talk about your transition when you were ready to leave the league. How did that go down for you?*

At the time, I had played in the league for 12 years. I was 35 years old and had won games in Super Bowls, and then one day I realized that I couldn't play forever. One of the things that we fool ourselves with is we're going to keep playing and old age isn't going to catch up to us; we're always going to be in great shape. You think, retirement happens to other guys, but it's not going to happen to me. And a lot of times, you start thinking about the end of your career too late, when the end is near. So I started thinking about it right after I turned 30 because I realized at some point I had to stop—I knew I wasn't going to play until I was 40. I also knew that at some point, something was going to happen, whether it was an injury or something else. So I had to think, "What is it that I want to do?" I was prepared. I had done some TV work while I was playing, and my hope was that I would get into TV. I auditioned immediately after I was done playing. I have to say, that distraction was good. But then you settle in, guys start going back to training camp and minicamp and everyone is talking about the season —but you're not there.

No matter how much you prepare, it still hits you. And it hits you pretty hard. But, again, I was prepared. I saved money. I can't imagine how stressful that transition can be for someone who isn't prepared and didn't save money. Because, what are you going to do? Most of us aren't going to make the same amount of money we made playing. So I went into TV. What I realized was that everyone was great, but the TV was a competition too. Everyone wanted the same job. You basically are at the whim of your boss and my boss at CBS Sports kind of blew like the wind. I remember thinking that if I stayed there I was going to be under the scrutiny of one person's opinion that could determine the rest of my life.

I speak to a lot of former players. I tell all of them that the greatest asset they'll have while they're still playing until the day they retire is their brand. Your name. Your ability to say, "I'm going to call the CEO and meet with him," or "I'm going to invite him and his kids to a game and meet them afterward," or "I'm going to engage and invest my time in learning about companies that I find interesting." Current players have the ultimate power to get great seats or go on road trips or help their kids. When you're still playing you can have anyone any time if you want. I realized that so I started talking to a couple of guys in venture capital whom I met while still playing.

Having my own business taught me a couple of things.

1) I still had a locker room. There were guys I could talk to who had gone through the same issues I had and it always gave us experience to draw upon. We had all battled through adversity. We learned a ton of things during our career in athletics that applied to business.

2) I had guys who loved to compete so we found an arena to compete; we wanted to be the next Facebook or the next Google. We wanted to be the next great entrepreneurs. We wanted to be around people who were superstar players in technology. So in Silicon Valley it all just worked out. But we also realized what our skills were, where our shortcomings were; we were honest with ourselves and we built around that. There's no better feeling than knowing you have your own business. And just because you have money doesn't mean you're going to have a great restaurant or car dealership. You have to put in the work! It doesn't happen like magic, and you shouldn't trust just anyone to run everything for you. While you're still playing, leverage your downtime and create some friends and relationships in different industries that could be significant for you down the line.

## Adonal Foyle, MA, MBA

*What was the hardest part of walking away from the game?*

In the NFL, you have 16 weeks. Game day was the toughest because when it's football season, almost everywhere you go, people are watching football. It's always in your face. It's always there. Then, there's that voice in your head that says, "You can still do this. You can still get in shape and play." That voice lasted for about three or four years after I retired. There was a part of me that thought maybe I could make a comeback. But really, what for? Eventually, it's going to end, even with the greatest. We saw Michael Jordan go through it. We are seeing Kobe Bryant go through it now. It happens to everyone. The earlier you come to grips with it, the better. The first year was the worst because people would come up to me and say that I looked like I was in great shape and that I could still lace them up. Or something like, "You need to be back out there. Your team sure misses you." You smile, but inside it's just tearing you up. You're also thinking, "My life was so much easier when I just went to games. I didn't have any responsibilities."

When it comes to basketball, I think Magic Johnson set the bar. He was always a guy intrigued by business. He's a competitor. In football, Roger Staubach from the Dallas Cowboys was spectacular. He started his own real estate firm and subsequently sold it for several hundred million dollars. He was great with people, he loved competing and he found something besides football that served as a passion.

The reality is, you're never ever going to replace playing professional sports at the highest level. The adrenaline, the excitement, the challenge. You just have to realize that there are other great things too.

*What kind of coping skills helped you with your transition?*

I think asking yourself, "What are my fallback positions?" There are a lot of guys out there who aren't finishing college. I got my degree, so that helped. My wife of 28 years was there for me and understood what I was going through. Going at this alone is tough too because most guys don't have the ability to express how they're really feeling. So that was huge. I think faith is a large part for a lot of guys, too. Direction helps, although I didn't have the perfect sense of direction at the time. I think I had a direction, which was television. The worst thing to do is retire and then ask yourself, "What am I going to do now?"

**If you could travel back to five years prior to your retirement, what would you tell yourself?**

I would have told myself to research all the industries I was interested in. I'd be reaching out to CEOs, top business people, investors, and thought leaders, and I would have taken some time during the off-season to see if I could spend a day or week engaging them and understanding what drives them. I would have told myself to build relationships outside of my sport. The fallback for most guys is that 80% either want to be on TV or think they can become a coach or GM. The reality is that only 2% of those guys get that far. It's easy to become discouraged.

The biggest thing is, I would have taken the opportunity to learn while people still want to teach me. I would have put in some hours to not only develop relationships but learn how a business works because just having money and saying you're in the industry is pretty tough.

**In terms of finance, what should a player's first priorities be, e.g., investing in real estate, property, etc.?**

Players should have a portfolio approach. What exactly does that mean? One of the things I used to tell guys is anyone who is tr23ying to pursue you and wants to be your financial manager is the guy you should be running from. You want to go to people who don't have time for you. Those are the people that you want and that's how you start learning about how your money is working for you. The same thing happens to us in football. There are guys who think they're going to play forever so they spend their next year's contract. I was on teams where teammates didn't realize that they had to pay taxes at the end of the year. The worst thing is to spend, spend, spend, and then realize that you don't have a salary coming in next year. When you're playing, you think that you're going to be okay. But the minute you stop, you don't know what to do. Then, guys get divorced. Talk about an investment; paying spousal support sucks the life right out of these guys' accounts. It can be a shock.

I think having a bucket strategy where you take X amount out of each check and allocate that to your living expenses, bills, etc. As an athlete, maybe it's taking what you make in the first four or five years and putting that money in short-term treasuries to use while building your next career. Another bucket would be intermediate term bonds and some safe stocks (do your homework, especially when it comes to stocks!). Athletes want to be the trailblazers for earning the most on the next great stock but you have to watch out. There are a lot of slick salesmen out there who look like they're your friends and want you to trust them.

They'll say that you can make 50 times your money on this or that and a lot of players will jump on the bandwagon. I'm telling you, it's an easy way to lose a lot of money. So I would take a smaller percentage of all you save and put it in a third bucket. That bucket would be the risk capital. Swinging for the fences. Half court capital. I'd put it in a few different ventures if you really want to take some risk. But do it alongside smart, sophisticated investors. The toughest thing to acknowledge is that you don't have all the answers. A lot of guys will say, "I got this. I know what I'm doing." But the reality is, you *don't* "got" it. So what I still do to this day is follow the smart money. Learn who the smart people are, and figure out what they're investing in. Because they've been doing it for years and years and years. And instead of having ego or attitude, humble yourself and be smart. Plan a long trajectory of safe finances so you can enjoy the flexibility of investing without a wipeout destroying you.

*Winning the Transition Game*

### What three things surprised you most in your retirement?

The number one thing was how badly I missed the game. You take it for granted every day until it's not there anymore. I missed all the guys I played with. Just kicking it in the locker room, having fun, laughing at inside jokes and messing around, and the road trips. When it ends, at first you think it's okay but it's like a good part of you dies. I thought I had prepared well yet I was STILL surprised at how heavy that feeling was.

The second thing is that I learned it's a tough world to maneuver out there. When you're playing, people give you so much free stuff; free shirts, free shoes, free custom golf clubs. You get used to having the best clothes, having a shoe contract, ordering whatever you want on any menu, getting custom made golf clubs and free cruises. Then BANG, it's over. My second year out of the league, I paid $150 for Nikes. My first thought was, "Are you kidding me? This is ridiculous!" I was enraged. I also had to pay for my own dinners again. The "freebie bus" starts to trail off, and it trails off drastically.

The third thing surprised me because it happened when I had already been away from the game for years. During your playing years you have people surrounding you, pushing you in the right direction to achieve more, to be more. But will it be the same post-sport when the people around you push you to succeed, to be great? The short, blunt answer is no. It doesn't carry the same feeling. But I'm telling you: you can still compete. You can still watch the scoreboard. You can still enjoy yourself. You can still mix it up with your boys. It's pretty great. It's not like your life is coming to an end. There's a light at the end of the tunnel.

### Any final thoughts?

If you check your pride at the door, you'll be okay. Also, I wish the leagues were doing more to help players; even something as little as a quarterly support group. I believe the reason why they don't is because there is no financial benefit to the leagues.

*Adonal Foyle, MA, MBA*

## Kristi Yamaguchi
**Retired, Professional American Figure Skater**
**Active 1984-2002**

## Bret Hedican
**Retired, Professional Hockey Player**
**Active 1991-2009**

*Talk about your respective sports. Why were you intrigued by that sport, and why did you choose your sport as a way of life?*

**Kristi:** When I was young, I think what enraptured me the most about figure skating was the performance. As a six-year-old, it just looked magical on the ice. The performances, the lights, the music, the costumes. And when I tried it, there was just an incredible sense of freedom on the ice. I was kind of a small, scrawny kid. An individual sport worked well for me because of my size and I didn't have to go head-to-head with anyone. It was about my own abilities. It gave me confidence. So for me, being a shy kid and learning how to work hard and accomplish things and be rewarded definitely helped give me confidence. Later on, my competitive nature started to come out; I wanted to beat people and be better than them.

**Bret:** For me, growing up in Minnesota, hockey is just what we did. Growing up, an outdoor park was just a block away from where I lived. There was a rink there that they watered every weekend. It would freeze over and that's where we'd spend our time all weekend long. My mom would come and drop off lunch in the snowbank.

She'd check to make sure we were still alive because we would play all day at the park, and not eat for 12 hours. That's just what we did. We'd play hockey in the winter, football in the fall, baseball in the spring and then back to hockey again. I didn't really know I'd grow up to become a professional hockey player. I never even imagined it. My pace was a bit more gradual. I was small as a kid and I didn't really grow until I was 17 years old. I grew seven inches in one year. Suddenly, I became this kid who could play hockey. Before, nobody really noticed me—they would say I was good, but I wasn't very big. Now I was 6-feet-2 yet I could still do the same things I was able to do when I was smaller.

One school, St. Cloud State, gave me a partial scholarship. They brought in 10 players that year, all freshmen, to kick off the program. That was really the break of a lifetime for me. It was my chance. It wasn't much, but I took it. I'd played defense my whole life, but I was recruited as a forward, a position I had never played before. It was a big transition for me but it was the one chance that got me going.

***Kristi, what did you enjoy about your sport, and what aspect did you not like?***

**Kristi:** Early on, it was just fun. The tough years were probably the teenage years, where in junior high and high school, the sacrifices become greater. There was obviously more training time and our ice time was all in the morning before school. I would wake up at 4 am and be on the ice by 5 am until 10-11 am. Then, I'd rush off to school. I'd spend part of my time on campus and another part doing independent studies. So it was a grueling schedule. Obviously, that meant I didn't have much of a social life because I was in bed every night at 7:30 pm.

I skated six days a week, so it was pretty intense. For me, it wasn't a huge sacrifice. This was what a competitor skater does. It was what I needed to do if I wanted to be a competitive skater. My fellow skaters were in the same boat. We all dealt with it and that was our life. In high school, I missed out on a lot. But I traded that for international travel and making friends in the skating world, who became lifeline friends for me. So there were tradeoffs for sure, but as an athlete, it's worth it. When you have that end goal and big dream, it's worth going for it.

Preparing for the Olympics was intense, but I thought I was really good at having a singular focus toward doing everything I had to do in order to prepare for that one moment. You're so honed in. You, your family, your coaches, everyone around you are all focused on that one Olympic year. And you don't think about what happens after that year so it's a pretty huge wake-up call afterwards.

**Bret, when everyone was paying attention to you, did you see that as an opportunity to take your skills to the next level?**

**Bret:** Not really. Not right away. My freshman year I was in and out of the lineup as a forward. Again, I had never played that position. In fact, in the first rink we practiced in, before they built the new one, there's a little corner where there was a cassette player that would play music while we were practicing. And for the players who weren't playing, it was their job to push the play button when the music stopped playing. I was one of those guys who had to push the play button. That was me, my freshman year.

For me, I still looked at it as an opportunity. I didn't stop believing in myself. At the end of that year, I went back to the coach's office and told him, "I am not a forward. I've been a defenseman my whole life. It's what I know. It's what I love about hockey. Seeing the ice in front of me, making great passes, stopping people one-on-one. It's what I loved to do as a kid. I want to come back next year as a defenseman, I can help this team on defense." He responded, "Oh. Go home, train all summer on defense and we'll see you next year." That was all he said.

My roommates and teammates thought I was going to get cut. But when I came back, I made the team, and I started scoring goals. So they could see right off that I could play defense. That's who I was. That year, I scored 17 points in 20 games and I kept progressing. But the next year was when everything really started coming together for me (as a junior). I scored 21 goals in 45 games as a defenseman. After the season, I was on spring break. I got a call from my mom and dad. They had just got a call from the United States National Team;

they were sending a team over to Russia to play in a four-country tournament. I'll never forget that call. It was the call of a lifetime. It was like, "Holy cow, this is it. This is my moment. This is what I've been waiting for." My mom and dad were crying on the phone.

I flew home the next day, got my equipment, joined the team in Boston, flew to Russia, and had four of the best games of my life. I just knew that this was *that* moment in time. The coaches for those four games during the tournament were the coaches of the next Olympic team. They asked me to try out for the National Olympic team the following summer—I made the team. My senior year I had to leave school because we traveled around the world and played with the national team. Just before the Olympics, we were in Germany and they selected the actual Olympic team a week before the games, and again, I made the team.

After the games, I went back to school. The quarter was supposed to start that following Monday. I had missed the first two quarters of the school year because I was playing. When the new quarter started, I skipped school on Monday and Tuesday because I thought I was going to get a call from the St. Louis Blues. No call.

On Wednesday, it's 8 am and I'm in class, thinking I wasn't going to go pro that year. Around noon, I put a pizza in the oven—and I got the call. The St. Louis Blues wanted to sign me. Next thing you know, I was on a plane, joined the team in Montreal, and played my first game in Toronto. Kristi says you don't really prepare for the next chapter in your life as far as professional sports goes but I think you just become goal oriented, you believe in yourself as a way of life. And if you do, who knows? Miracles can happen.

*Kristi, what do you remember about your first Olympics?*

**Kristi:** You're so proud to say that you're not just a skater anymore. I thought, "Now, I'm representing my country. I can wear the red, white and blue and it means something." It's really humbling and an honor at the same time. I thought that was the most important thing. At that point, I was thinking, "Whatever happens at the Olympics, great, but I made my ultimate goal of becoming an Olympian."

I trained as hard as I could, I was hoping that I would just compete well. I thought if I could do that, I'd have a chance to win. If not, I'd keep competing and maybe try out for the next Olympics. So it was intense and it felt like walking on eggshells for a year. You want everything to be going perfectly and you want to peak at the right time. It's not like a basketball season where you play 82 games. With each figure skating competition, you're building on each performance, on each routine.

**Bret, talk about the arc of your career once you made it to the NHL. What did you enjoy about playing at that level, and what did you dislike?**

**Bret:** For me, the greatest thing to ever happen to me was my first couple of years... when I was miserable. I was not in a good team environment. When you come from college hockey (probably like in any sport), there's a camaraderie that lasts forever. It's a bond that you have with your teammates. In college, there's only a couple of things you worry about: you go to class and you play hockey. You have fun while learning about life, you do a lot of growing up; you learn very fast that you're responsible for your own food and laundry, and cleaning your own apartment, etc.

You just learn about life. I thought that was what was so great about college. When I got to the NHL, the first couple of years were miserable because there was no unity among the teammates. There was jealousy. Certain guys were upset about their teammates scoring goals. I thought, "This is not right. This is not a good environment. I hope this is not what the NHL is all about. Maybe this is just not a good team." I remember calling my dad and telling him, "If this is what the NHL is all about, I don't want anything to do with it. I'll go back to school."

My dad told me to hang in there and maybe something will happen. He said, "Just keep working on your game and believe in yourself." It was a good call because I listened to him and stayed in it. A year later, I get a call and I hear that I got traded to a team that we just played against, a game where I got into a fight with one of their players. I joined that team and it was exactly what I imagined an NHL team to be—a bunch of hard-working guys. They were a bunch of good guys and it was exactly what the environment was like on the inside. That team, the Carolina Hurricanes, went all the way to the Stanley Cup Finals. We lost in the finals, but what that experience taught me was when you know you're at the bottom of the arc, you know it's got to get better and there has to be a better way to function as a team.

When I got traded to the Hurricanes, I finally knew what a good environment was like. And throughout my career, even when I was hitting some dips, I was always searching for a good environment. And that's what I continue to search for today beyond sports. I'm always looking for an environment that creates a healthy place for people to thrive in what they do and make sure everyone feels important to the team. Those are the qualities that you look for beyond sports that are important.

**When you look back at your career, what were the three high points?**

**Kristi:** Probably when I was 16 years old. I went to the World Junior Championships. At the time, I was seen as a pairs skater, but this was the first time I competed as a pairs skater *and* a single skater. I ended up winning the singles event AND the pairs event. At that point, the skating world was wondering, "Who IS this girl?" So that was kind of my coming out party. My second big moment was during the 1991 World Championships. I had a tough year. Just a few months prior to the championships, I was literally thinking about if I still wanted to skate. I was miserable. But I had a wakeup call and did a 180-degree turn as far as my attitude and perspective. I wanted to do things my way. And that gave me the power, emotionally, to enjoy skating again and it made a huge difference. So I went on to win my first World Championship that year, and with 1991 being a pre-Olympic year, it set me up in a nice position for the Olympics.

**Bret:** When you win at the highest level and you feel what that feels like (along with the work it takes to get there), compared to other championship teams I was on that didn't win. The pinnacle of winning during that celebration, along with the other 25 guys you've been working with to get there, that is a moment where you will always say, "THAT is what you play for." THAT'S what I worked for as a kid. Winning a Stanley Cup championship is the pinnacle.

Feeling what it feels like when you're at your best. When you're trained, when you're physically fit at the highest level, and then being able to go on the field, court or ice rink and execute at the highest level. That is a great feeling. Athletes want to feel that again. And when they retire, they know they will never feel that again; feeling their best, being at their best and executing at their best. You have to train and be mentally ready for all those things.

The third thing that stands out for me is when I finally realized the mental side of sports. That was a game changer for me. I had a tough coach that exposed a lot of weaknesses in me at the NHL level. And although it was really difficult to go through, it taught me more about myself than any other skills I ever learned. When that coach traded me and gave up on me, it was like getting stabbed in the heart. I think every athlete has felt that at some point in his or her life. It was a great transition because I knew that nobody would ever control my mind again. That's when I started doing more mental repetitions and positive reinforcements. Kristi is a really good person to ask about this because she had to do it individually, while I had to do it with a team. But you can overcome so much by executing on the mental side.

*When did you experience that "ah-ha" moment when you realized your career was going to end?*

**Kristi:** Luckily after the Olympics, I still skated so I felt like I had an extended career as a professional skater after my competitive years. Although that was great, I knew it could only last for so long. I had toured for 10 years, and at that point, Bret and I had been married for almost two years. I was sick of the road and I didn't want to live out of a suitcase anymore. I wanted to be in one spot. I was preparing for that moment all season because I knew it was the last year of my contract. And everyone else knew, too. I didn't want to have a big farewell tour because I was afraid of the whole idea of shutting that door, but I have to say, my last tour was a very special tour. Every night during that final year, I just soaked in standing on the ice and hearing the crowd cheer. Every performance was special and I knew I had to enjoy it. During my last performance, it was surreal because I didn't know what the other side was going to be like. I was excited about leaving, but I was going to miss it. And I knew that nothing in the world was going to replace that atmosphere. So it was a little scary with a lot of anxiety along the way but I was looking forward to my next chapter.

That first month of normalcy was kind of liberating. I felt like, "Wow, I don't have to worry about what I'm eating, how much sleep I get, or how much I train every day." For a moment it felt like I was going to be on vacation for the rest of my life. But you do get to a point where you need purpose. You need a reason to get up in the morning. Fortunately for me, I was ready to start a family and I knew that would carry its own life transition. Anytime you look at motherhood, it's scary but exciting. I was ready. Outside of starting a family, though, I knew I still needed some challenge in my life. And then there's that inevitable transitional question: what am I going to do next? What's going to happen to me? It's funny because I kind of stepped into Bret's world and became a wife and mother. I think I had to get out of skating completely in order to do that. I stayed in touch with my friends and colleagues, and I think I needed to do that in order to make the transition. It also helped me get back involved in the sport in a different way.

**Bret:** I think women athletes have an advantage in making the transition out of sports, especially those who want to start a family, because if they're pregnant, their careers are put on pause. Kristi was able to focus on being a wife and mother while I was still playing. So the time away from her sport to start a family really helped Kristi with her transition out of figure skating. For me, when the end was near, I knew I was ready. I knew I wanted to retire.

At that point, I had played 17 seasons. That's more than 1,000 games. I had had enough. I didn't want to go out there and take a beating anymore. And even though I could probably grind through another season, if I played four games a week, I could probably give you three good games, but that fourth game would be a nightmare for me; it wouldn't be any fun. But at the same time, even though I knew I was ready, I wasn't ready, if that makes sense.

I attended school for a while at Cal and the University of San Francisco but that really wasn't enough of a challenge for me. I loved it, but it wasn't what I was really looking for. I started getting involved with different businesses as well as the U.S. Olympic team.

***Do you remember thinking about what retirement was going to be like, and then actually experiencing it for the first time?***

**Kristi:** You feel unfulfilled. You want to keep something in you. I actively looked for other things to do. In 1996, I started the Always Dream Foundation. That gave me focus and purpose. I had to learn how to not be a part of the sport, but more of a fan of the sport. And I can say that I really am a fan now. I want to support the skaters and still find a way to make a difference in our sport.

At one point, U.S. Figure Skating realized that they had an abundance of assets but weren't using them. They enlisted a lot of us former skaters to reach out to young skaters and offer mentoring; we were available to the other skaters whenever they wanted advice. I also started hosting and emceeing different shows for skating.

***Kristi, talk about your writing and what it means to you. For me, writing and reading to kids really helped me, and I know it has helped you too.***

**Kristi:** I always knew that I wanted to do something that focused on children. That's how my foundation was founded. I had always had that feeling of wanting to write a children's book one day. When Bret and I had our children, the doctor told us to start reading to her as a baby. The doctor said it was good for our daughter to hear our voices and for us to show her pictures from the book. So that's what we did. By the time she was two or three years old, we were still reading the same book over and over again. I started to think, "How many times can we read Goodnight Moon?"

That's when I thought it was a good time to write a book for her. Our children were about four and two when I wrote the book, and I realized just how important it was to spend time with the kids. At the same time, it was good to share the process of writing the book with them so I tried to make them feel a part of the process. I had fun sharing my book with other kids, going to schools, reading to kids in classrooms, and seeing their reactions. That really opened up my eyes on how the power of a simple children's book can get them interested in reaching for another book, and another. The next step was to focus on the foundation, which emphasizes the importance of childhood literacy.

*Adonal Foyle, MA, MBA*

**Bret, if you were able to provide a fellow athlete some coping mechanisms for retirement, based on what you went through, what would you advise?**

**Bret:** I think it was the two-year mark when I started to think, "How do I start letting go?" Even though I was ready to retire, I didn't let it go emotionally, mentally, or even physically. Wanting to be physically fit all the time, training seven days a week, has to go by the wayside. You have to try to be a dad and be there for your wife and kids. You need to find ways to get balanced again. When it comes to getting ready for retirement, I don't know if every person is going to fit into one "do it this way" mold.

Players should really find something they can sink their teeth into. They might not find it right away, but there are workshops that can help. If there's a business you're interested in, but you're not too familiar with how it operates, a workshop can help you understand what's involved. What we learn during our athletic careers is to not be afraid to fail. But you're going to fail and you're going to make mistakes. You learn at some point during your professional career that you have to get up the next day, put your gear on, and even though you cost your team the game last night, you have to come out and play well tomorrow. By doing that, you become a pro.

When you retire, you try different jobs and businesses and you may fail at that too. But you have to learn, the same way you learned as a pro: you're going to fail. But you have to shake it off, get to the next day and keep going, keep pushing toward where you want to go. It's a key pivotal moment that we forget; we failed a lot as a pro so there's nothing wrong with failing in your next career.

# Roy Byrd
**Former Harlem Globetrotter**
**Active 1998–2003**

*What does basketball mean to you?*

I can't even put it into words. Basketball is a sport that you live for and die for. It's an amazing feeling when you're able to run up and down the court, with 20,000 people watching you do something you love. It's a great feeling.

*Looking back at your basketball career, what stands out to you the most?*

All the hard work when I'm out in the gym or on the playground getting shots up and working out. Being able to sign my contract showed me that all my hard work had paid off. When I signed that contract, my dream finally came through. I didn't know what to do. So the first thing I did was call my mom (collect). I told her that I just signed with the Harlem Globetrotters. She said, "Good, you can pay for this phone call."

*When you look at your career with the Globetrotters, summarize what that experience was like.*

Traveling to different states and countries to perform in front of thousands of fans was great. I was born in Germany and I was able to return to Europe and go on tour. I walked the Great Wall of China and went to NORAD. Those are things I wouldn't have been able to do if it weren't for the Harlem Globetrotters. So I really felt blessed to be able to do what I was doing.

*Adonal Foyle, MA, MBA*

*What are some of your standout on-the-court memories?*

My first year, I played at Madison Square Garden. It took me back to when the Chicago Bulls played the New York Knicks and how loud the crowd got when Michael Jordan was in town. I pictured Spike Lee sitting courtside. We played in a building that had a lot of history, and I will never forget performing in front of the fans at Madison Square Garden. We normally start playing the first five minutes of every quarter, and the coach calls out the play to start the show. I was still in basketball mode. My first shot was an NBA three-pointer. You could not stop me for those five minutes. That's one highlight I'll never forget.

*You were born in Germany, raised in Oakland, and played for the Harlem Globetrotters. When you started out, could you even comprehend that journey?*

No. Growing up in Germany, there are flat lands everywhere; it's a different country. Everybody knew everybody, and you could go to sleep with your door wide open. Everybody is nice and friendly. In 1978, my life changed and I relocated from Germany to Oakland, California. I moved to the ghetto where there were 10 locks on the doors, and you definitely could not leave the windows open. It was a completely different world and I didn't know how to adjust so I had to basically become one of the people in the neighborhood who just wanted to get out of there. When you live in that type of neighborhood, you either become a drug dealer or killer, or be killed. At the time it had never crossed my mind that I would someday play for one of the most recognizable basketball organizations in the world, the Harlem Globetrotters; they were the very first team I saw on TV.

*How long did you play for the Globetrotters?*

From 1998 to 2003.

***During your playing days, did the thought cross your mind on what you would do in your post-playing career?***

I had an idea of what I wanted to do once I retired, but I was not able to put my idea to use. I always wanted to dabble in the real estate market, buying properties and apartment buildings. Before I could do that, my career was cut short and I was forced into retirement. That was my struggle.

***What forced you to retire?***

I was a goodwill ambassador for the team. That involved going around and talking about the team on TV or radio, and I also made appearances in schools and hospitals. Then I would go back to the team and play. We went back to Oakland for a performance and we visited my former elementary school. I was talking to the kids about how I wasn't LeBron James, Kobe Bryant or Kevin Garnett. I wasn't someone who went straight from high school to the Harlem Globetrotters. My dream came 10 years after high school. Within those 10 years, I had a lot of jobs. I worked at FedEx on the ramp, I was a garbage man hanging on the back of a smelly truck.

I was supposed to go to Patten College but things didn't work out there so I went back to the garbage company. When I was telling the kids this story, I told them that hanging on the back of the garbage truck wasn't fun. A reporter was in the classroom, writing a story about what I was saying. There were some inaccuracies in the story that put Patten College in a bad light. Patten got wind of the story and called the Globetrotters and said they were upset with the story.

The Globetrotters accused me of lying about my background (the story said I played for Patten College, but that was not true). Before I signed with the Globetrotters, I told them that I played there during the summer, but I did not play a single season for them. Basically, the Globetrotters suspended me 90 days without pay and I was up for a

*Adonal Foyle, MA, MBA*

contract renewal. They came to me with an offer they knew I wasn't going to take. So I was forced into retirement and walked away. It was the biggest mistake I ever made—I didn't stay there and fight for myself.

**What was it like the next morning when you realized that you were a FORMER Harlem Globetrotter?**

It took me back to being eight years old. Because again, I was born in Germany in 1970, came to Oakland California when I was eight years old, and my life changed overnight. When the Globetrotters and I parted ways, I felt like I was on a roller coaster ride again. The experience took me back to how I felt when I moved out of Germany. I had been on top of the world, now I was on the ground. Up in the air, and then back down again. I was in a tailspin for a while. That's not a happy place. You can make a big deal out of the smallest things because you're angry inside and you take it out on everyone else. But the only person you have to fault is yourself.

Not a lot of people can make an easy transition, and because being a basketball player, you're in a different world. To come out of our world and go into a different world, it's not easy. I wasn't aware of all the new technologies in the world, and I wasn't ready to delve into even simple things, because I was a ballplayer and all I knew how to do was go out and perform in front of fans and travel around the world. To just come home and sit there and think about what I was going to do next when I didn't have an answer to that question—it was easy to become an angry person.

**How did your anger manifest itself?**

I could be driving down the street and see someone with a clear lane in front of them, and I would start yelling at them to get over. Or I would just get down on myself with self-doubts about not being able to get back to the level I was at before. Any little thing could set me off. Someone could say, "Good morning," and I would respond,

"What's good about it?" A number of things could happen and all of it just made me an angry person. It's a very dark place.

**What would you say were the three biggest changes you had to make when transitioning to a "regular" person?**

First, I was not making the same money I was used to getting so I started sinking deeper and deeper into a financial hole. Then I started asking myself how I would continue to live every single day while trying to climb out of a hole at the same time. That's hard. The second challenge was going from someone who was always asked to sign an autograph or make an appearance to having none of that happen anymore. During my transition, I didn't know what to do. Third, I doubted myself a lot, wondering if I would *ever* get back to where I was. It was just a really, really hard time in my life.

**What do you miss most about playing for the Harlem Globetrotters?**

I miss running out of that tunnel and having all the eyes on me when I was at center court. I miss playing basketball and listening to "Sweet Georgia Brown" (the Harlem Globetrotters theme song). I miss those nights after the game where people would come up to me and tell me stories about how when they were kids their parents brought them to games, and now they're taking their own kids to the games. I miss the bus rides with my teammates, and I miss the pranks we pulled on each other. One time I poured a bucket of ice water on a teammate while he was in the shower. I miss playing cards with my coach. Just the brotherhood. I miss all that.

**How long have you been out of your sport?**

About 12 years now.

*Adonal Foyle, MA, MBA*

***Looking back at those 12 years, how are you viewing your retirement now?***

For me, it hasn't been easy being in retirement. I wasn't ready to go. I felt like I was pushed out versus walking out on my own so I take that as something that's twice as hard to get over. And it has taken me twice as long, because although I know I'm a people person, I still don't know what else I'm good at, and that's very tough for me.

***How did your relationships with family and friends change after retirement?***

It took a toll on me. I was married at the time and it got to the point where I felt like I wasn't the provider anymore, like I wasn't the man of the house because I wasn't playing ball. It cost me my marriage and that made me unhappy because after we filed for divorce, I lost my home (I gave it to her). I got into another relationship, but I wasn't happy with that relationship. Basically, I had to take time and just work on Roy. What would make Roy happy? One thing that stuck in my mind was when I put that Globetrotters jersey on, I was Roy Byrd. When I took that jersey off, I was still Roy Byrd. I wanted to continue being Roy Byrd every single day. But to talk about it and do it at the same time was rough and tough. I could give advice, but sometimes it's harder to take your own advice.

***Was there anyone or anything that helped you in your transition?***

Yes. There was a person named Ronnie Brockhoff. Ronnie had known me since I was 15 years old. I constantly stayed on the phone with him while I was playing ball; I would tell him about certain things that made me unhappy. When I was forced into retirement, the other person who helped me was you—Adonal Foyle. You were constantly talking to me about what my next chapter in life was, and what else

I could do. You were always offering me a conversation, picking my brain, and pushing me to be the person that I am today. Those two people got me to 44 years old because some people in my situation would have either taken their own life or turned to drugs.

*At this point in your life, would you say you have turned a corner, or are you still struggling with your transition?*

I would say I'm at about 50-50 right now, and I can honestly say that I'm not angry about it anymore. I'm just more hurt about how my retirement happened, and it's not like I'm looking for the Globetrotters to come and apologize to me (that would never happen, anyway). But it's still part of my past. I know I have to move on from it, but I live my life still trying to figure out how to climb out of the hole I've been pushed into. That, for me, is still difficult every single day. I have yet to find the answer.

*How have your relationships evolved during retirement?*

My ex-wife and I are now able to communicate because we have a beautiful daughter together. When we split, our daughter was two years old. It's good to communicate again. My relationships with Ronnie and Adonal are great; they are my brothers and I love them to death. I will always cherish those relationships. I am remarried, and my wife, Kristen, is phenomenal.

*What kind of coping strategies did you employ in the last eight years to help you through your retirement?*

What worked for me was to forgive. I forgave the Globetrotters because I didn't want to be a prisoner to the situation. Then, it was about starting the healing process. When that ends, I have no idea but I do know that every day is still a battle.

*Adonal Foyle, MA, MBA*

**For an athlete who is now considering retirement, what would you share with him regarding the most challenging aspect of retirement?**

One of the most difficult things to get over is the reality that you won't be hanging around with your teammates anymore. When you're on a team, you form a bond. You can still have it beyond your playing days, but it won't be the same. The second thing is the money. You need to have your ducks in a row BEFORE you retire. You can't think that you can still live the same lifestyle after you're done playing and expect the same money to come in. Otherwise, you'll wind up being angry, frustrated... and broke.

**Is it hurtful to see other guys moving forward while you're still trying to figure things out?**

Sometimes. Those guys weren't forced into retirement like I was. Several of them left on their own. So, again, if I was able to leave on my own terms, I would have the same mindset as they have.

**If you had to do it all over again, what would you do differently?**

To be honest with you—and this might sound crazy—but nothing. Because I was able to fulfill my dream, and like I said, it wasn't the NBA. My mom once told me, "That job fitted me. It fitted my attitude and it brought people to me. Considering what the Harlem Globetrotters stood for in history, it was great. The only thing I wish was that there were different people in the organization.

**Is there anything you'd like to add?**

Being in retirement has its good days and bad days but I think all in all, I've had many more good days than bad days. But it's still a struggle every single day. And I think it will always be, but I'm able to control it a little better now.

## J.J. Stokes
Retired, NFL Wide Receiver
Active 1995-2003

*Talk about the process when the time came to retire and begin your transition.*

For me, I remember when the season was over and I'd work out during the summer and get ready for the next season. My wife, who was my girlfriend at the time, would ask me, "What are you going to do when you're done?" What I did while I was at UCLA was talk to some counselors about doing radio work. When I got drafted by the 49ers, I had my agent connect me with a local radio station. At the time, there was just one sports station in the Bay Area so I would do spots after the games. I was slowly doing something I thought I might be doing by the time I was done playing. Knowing what I know now, though, I would have done more of it during the summer as a working internship. It would have been nice to be behind the scenes in radio to create a smoother transition. That's probably how I would have changed things.

When the end was near and I got released by the New England Patriots, I came back to the Bay Area; I had a few buddies who knew some local radio show hosts so I spent a little time working with the stations in the Bay Area and Sacramento. But I also knew a guy who knew some radio personalities in Modesto. Turns out they needed a guy to fill a spot and it helped that I was a former NFL player because it would draw listeners. That was my immediate transition. Now, I was doing radio twice a week. I would travel from the Bay Area to Modesto to do a radio show that was just an hour and a half long. I knew it was something I loved to do because there's no compensation that would make me travel all the way to Modesto just to do a 90-minute radio show twice a week. I did that for a few months and it eventually turned into an everyday show in the afternoons from 12-3 pm. As my partner and I got better, we switched to the afternoon slot, which was 3-6 pm. Those are peak hours because that's the afternoon drive home.

Things were running pretty smoothly. I wound up as a host on the show for two years. One day as I was getting ready to go to work, my partner calls me and says I don't need to come in anymore. Turns out, the housing market had crashed, which meant we lost a lot of advertising and we were no longer on the air. I remember thinking, "What am I going to do now?" I wanted to devise a plan to get back on radio or TV. I had a relationship with the folks at Sports Byline USA (internet based) in San Francisco, and we knew that a station was going to open up that was going to be the flagship station for the Oakland A's. So we pitched them the idea of having a show, and it worked.

Around that same time I got a call from ESPN to be part of a documentary about Jerry Rice. I talked about Jerry and they were really impressed by how we were able to do it all in one take. I told them that I had been spending a lot of time doing radio. I was then referred to an agent named Debbie Spander, who lives in Southern California. We hit it off really well and the next thing I knew, I started working for Fox Sports Net on the weekends. That was my transition from radio to TV (plus, the flagship station for the A's went bankrupt shortly after I started so I was very fortunate to have transitioned to TV).

*My track record after playing football has been based on the relationships that I have developed over the years. I didn't treat anyone badly along the way.*

Working with Debbie was great, and I was fortunate to have developed a lot of other relationships along the way. Eventually, the Fox Sports Net opportunity dried up too. So this past year I have been coaching high school football at Bishop O'Dowd in Oakland, along with Napoleon Kaufman, who I played against both in college and in the NFL. My track record after playing football has been based on the relationships that I have developed over the years. I didn't treat anyone badly along the way.

But it is still difficult. Yes, it's definitely difficult. Because everyone wants to be around you when you're playing. But when you're not playing, they just move on to the guy who's still playing. Life after professional sports continues to be about communication. I still like to talk to people. As far as the people who ended contact with me after I retired, they might as well lose my number.

**Talk about your career in the NFL. How long were you in the league? What did you enjoy about the game and what was terrible about it?**

I played nine years in the NFL; eight of those years were with the San Francisco 49ers. I played half a season with the Jacksonville Jaguars and another half with the New England Patriots. When it comes to the good times, with the 49ers, obviously everything is so much better when you're winning. Of my eight years playing, six were winning seasons. But there were also two horrible seasons. Mentally, we tried to push harder to get a better result, but nothing came of it. We were still losing games.

It's like a ball rolling down a hill. Once it started rolling, nobody could stop it. And that's never fun. We tried to use it to motivate us. We would practice more, we'd watch more film, and we'd lift more weights. But on Sunday, it just wasn't fun because the hard work we put in didn't show. I hated losing. I always felt like when you lose, there's something you can do about it. And when you can't do anything about it, you feel helpless.

Going to Jacksonville was probably the worst decision I ever made. I had opportunities to go to Denver or Green Bay but I chose Jacksonville because through my life as a player, there was never a time where I wasn't a starter or the focal point of the offense. Green Bay offered me a backup role, and Denver offered the same. Even though those situations were better, I chose to go to Jacksonville because I was going to be a starter. At the time, the circumstance was good. But when I got there, it was a false circumstance. One of the receivers got popped for drugs and our quarterback wasn't as healthy as he could have been. So looking back, it was a bad decision. All I wanted to do was be a starter and have an opportunity to continue.

As far as the fun times go, you come to work and you practice with the guys. You're enjoying the good times. But what was most important was winning. For me, it was going to work, talking smack with the guys and being part of an atmosphere that was uncensored; we were in an uncensored world where we could go out, lift weights, run around, be physically fit, and have camaraderie with the guys. The games were easier than practice. And that was because we had an older team.

When I got to the Patriots, I could see why they were so successful—they were a well-oiled machine. Everything is about their process. They're so structured. They can plug anyone into their spots, and whoever they plug in can do the single thing they want them to do. Their practices were sharp, they paid attention to detail, and it reminded me of my first four years with the 49ers. The only thing I didn't like about being on the Patriots was practicing in 10-degree weather in the winter. I'm a Southern California kid. But it wasn't just me, the whole team felt that way.

If there is anything I could change in my career, it would be just a couple of decisions I made. I would have worked harder during the off-season and I would not have signed with Jacksonville.

## *What did being a football player mean to you?*

I should start by saying I have three older brothers. They're 12, 11, and 10 years older than me. When I was born, my dad and my brothers were all watching football. So I was watching football too. I fell in love with it, so I started playing football when I was seven. There was a trickle-down effect and I played the game because I loved it. And I think I loved it because my family loved it. My brothers played football too. It was just something that we did.

I didn't necessarily see football as a way to "make it." What was different for me was that I loved playing, through the good years and even during the bad years. But when football becomes a business, it's different. Even in college, it felt different because it wasn't just a game anymore. Even though there were some political things going on, I kept my grades up and I got on the field. My first season in the NFL, things were even more different because now it was professional ball. My first year in the league, I was naive. I was getting my feet wet, trying to understand how everything worked together. As I got older, I got it.

When I was younger and I watched college and NFL games, I used to think how lucky all those players were. And don't get me wrong. There are more great things than bad things. But when you get to the pro level, you realize that it's not just about being good and carrying yourself the right way. I've been on teams where the coaches had relationships with other players' fathers. I used to always wonder, are we trying to win games, or are we just cultivating relationships? That aspect took away from how I felt about football at the professional level. That part disgusted me.

*Adonal Foyle, MA, MBA*

**At what point did you realize that your professional football career was over?**

When I got released by the Patriots in 2003, I came home nursing an injury. So my first thought was to nurse my injury so I could get back on the field. My agent told me that my type of injury took about a month to recover from. But I didn't want to wait that long because no other team would bring me in for a workout. So I worked with a trainer and tried to come back sooner.

The New Orleans Saints called me in for a workout. If I had postponed it, they weren't going to call back. So I worked out with the Saints and the first thing they asked me to do was run a 40-yard dash. So I'm nursing an injured quad and hamstring which was the last thing I wanted to do. I think I ran a 4.6 or 4.7 in the 40 (and I hadn't run that since high school). Then I started running routes for them and was catching the ball. At the end of the day, they thought I was great, but I ended up not signing with them.

Before the 2004 season, I went through a period when I switched agencies. My new agent got me a workout with the Buffalo Bills. It was the only workout I had. I was going to make the time, or it might be time for me to hang it up. It turned out that my chances of making the team at Buffalo depended on what their plans were for another receiver on the team. And he had been *The Man* on that team for a long time. I figured they were going to give him more respect than someone new like me. So it didn't work out in Buffalo.

That year, I wanted to stay in shape in case someone called. At the same time, that's when the radio opportunities started coming in. So I would work out in the morning, then do radio in the afternoon.

The realization of walking away really hit me after my workout with Buffalo. I was just a few months removed from being on a team, and nobody was calling anymore, as opposed to when I was a free agent and my agent would tell me how many teams were interested, and I got to choose which teams I wanted to look into.

**When did you know you were done for real?**

It's funny because the next year, during Thanksgiving, I was at my in-laws' house; we were having drinks that night. My agent called and told me he might have a workout for me. I called my trainer so I could work out that night. I had some wine in me so I was sipping water all night. We wound up working out at midnight, and it was intense.

> *"When you start hoping and wishing, you might as well call it a day."*

I realized just how out of shape I was. We worked out for about a month and a half straight. My agent called me one day to let me know that the team had passed. When he told me they passed, I started to think, "There's no need to live like this." One of my old coaches, George Stewart, once said, "When you start hoping and wishing, you might as well call it a day." And when that team passed, that's exactly when I remembered Stewart's words: I was hoping and wishing. That's not me. That's not who I am. I knew I was done.

**Once you made that decision, what was the next day like?**

It's funny because once I made the decision, I started saying, "I'm not going to even think about going back." I sat around the house, I did my radio gig, but not much else. At one point, I felt pathetic, and I stayed pathetic for six months. Even though I was on the radio, it felt different. I would have dreams about teams calling me, being back in shape, and playing again. The first year out of football, I watched games and felt like, "I could make that catch. How did he miss that?" The second year, I would say, "Coach has got to do a better job teaching him that move."

By the third year, I started to think, "Man, I'm sure glad I'm not getting hit like that anymore." Once I got to THAT point (2006), I realized the fan in me started coming out again. That was three years after my last game. I still love the game. I went to my very first tailgate and I admit, I didn't even know how to act during a tailgate. People were drinking and eating and talking. So I grabbed a cold one and relaxed with everyone else. I think, though, that my ah-ha moment came when I was at that tailgate. I realized I didn't have any worries. I was relaxing, eating, drinking and getting ready to watch a game. It took me three years to feel comfortable about being retired. Now, when I'm watching a game, I'm no longer saying, "I could have done that."

*Being away from football, how do you define happiness today?*

I have a six-year-old daughter and wife of 12 years so for me, a happy moment today can be really simple. I could be teaching my daughter how to play chess or checkers or it could be all of us playing a game and having a good time. We could be relaxing while going on vacation, going out to dinner, or sitting in the backyard by the fire and roasting some marshmallows. Those are things that are fun and happy now. Don't get me wrong. I still have those moments where I invite the fellas over and I'll get on the grill and smoke some meat. Those are good times. But I also associate myself with people who have kids the same age as my daughter. My daughter plays lacrosse and basketball and it's fun to be involved with our kids' activities.

*Talk to your younger self about preparing for retirement.*

I would tell my 23-year-old self about the mistakes I made when it came to preparation. I would tell him the mistakes I made when it came to finances; how to be cautious and skeptical of everybody—even if it's someone close to you. Because they're out there to make their money and they don't care if it's at your expense (I had a personal experience with that).

Regarding retirement, I would tell him to be prepared, how to really cultivate the relationships that are created while playing because you really don't know when your last game is going to be. Have a plan now. A pro career can last many years, or less than one year.

I would tell my younger self to find something he loves doing while he's still playing so he doesn't wind up scrambling and looking for something to do after he's done.

*What about you? Did you find what you love to do?*

I think so. I always wanted to be around football—I enjoy discussing the game. I've started football camps for kids. For me, that's fun, especially when they're young because they're always having ah-ha moments when they're coming up in the game. So I have fun with the kids and I have fun seeing them progress. The school where I coach, I think the kids are over-the-top appreciative. I've had kids tell me that I changed the way they see things, or that I changed their whole attitude. I told my wife how surprised I was to hear some of the things they were telling me. I could get used to that.

*When you thought about retirement, were those thoughts mostly positive, or mostly negative?*

My thoughts were POSITIVE. When I thought about retirement, I thought, "I'm going to stay home, sit on my butt and just hang out." My first thoughts were that I'm going to do whatever I wanted to do, but that wasn't the case.

*Adonal Foyle, MA, MBA*

**What was the reality?**

It wasn't like that at all. There's never a dull moment in this family. We're always doing something. We're always busy.

**What role did the league play in terms of your transition?**

The league continues to do things that help with transition. They have round robins around Super Bowl time that provides opportunities to speak to businesses. They offer boot camps if you want to become a franchisee, get into music production, or be in front of a camera. They have everything. They offer classes at Stanford about entrepreneurship. Transitioning players need to know that there are things available for you as a player.

I wish they had those offerings while I was still playing, although it benefits me to participate in them now. If I had had the opportunity to go to Stanford for three weeks, I know I would have signed up.

**If you had to do it all over again, what would you do differently?**

I would have been married by the time I was 26, and I would have worked in the off-season. I would have bought more real estate early on. My wife was in real estate and she was telling me to do that while I was playing. I should have listened.

## Ryan-Thomas Brown
Veteran, US Marine Corps
Active 2011-2014

*What made you want to join the military?*

My reasons for wanting to join the military are multi-faceted. My dad's step-father was in the Army before he passed away. Toward the end of his life, he was starting to lose it, mentally. But whenever he was coherent, it was always while he was telling me military stories. I really loved that about him. I still remember it like it was yesterday. We didn't have a lot of money, so we would buy those small cans of Vienna sausages and eat those while he was telling me his stories.

About two or three years after he passed away, I attended a wedding for my uncle in Bakersfield. There were a bunch of Marines sitting at the bar. I walked up to them and thanked them for their service. One of the Marines asked his commanding officer if he could give me his Eagle, Globe, and Anchor. In the Marines, that's a big deal. You're not a Marine during training. You become one once you are given the Eagle, Globe, and Anchor. And for someone to take their personal Eagle, Globe, and Anchor, and give it to a civilian, it meant a lot. It also meant a lot to the Marine that someone like me appreciated his gesture. At the time, I didn't realize what I was doing. The next day, those same Marines came to my room and wanted to hang out. They reserved a spot at the swimming pool and invited me to join them. Having grown up with a military family, I always thought about joining the military, and now, here I was hanging out with them.

After I graduated from high school, I got a nomination from my Congressman to attend a service academy, but was not accepted so I enlisted. First, I went to all the branches. When I walked to the Air Force, the women I was going to talk to was on the phone, so I told her I'd come back. The guys from the Navy were at lunch. When I walked into the Marine Corps, there was someone there. I still remember his name; Sgt. Brown. Great guy. He told me that he wasn't going to sit there and tell me the reasons why I should join the Marines. He said if I wanted to join the Marines, I should just do it. Then, he told me, "Get out of my office and don't come back unless you want to join the Marines."

When we left, my dad felt like the sergeant's comment was a bit unexpected. But I liked it. I thought it was a "man up" mentality. When I went to the Army, they all pretty much tried to jump me. I went back to the Navy and they were still at lunch. When I went to the Air Force, I was told it would take nine to ten months before I could even sign up. There was a huge wait list because everyone wanted to go to the Air Force because it was considered the safest during a time of war. I went back to my room and I saw that Eagle, Globe and Anchor sitting there. I looked at it and just said, "Fuck it." So I enlisted in the Marine Corps the next day.

*What was your journey like?*

I was in the Marine Corps for about four years. It's actually more difficult to get into the Marines than you think. There's a whole process behind getting into the Marines: you have to pass drug evaluations and you have to take a written test. I was fortunate to score high enough to qualify for any job. You have to get full medical examinations and wait for the results to come back. They want to make sure you don't have any chronic diseases, etc.

*Based on your four years of service in the Marines, what is your overall assessment?*

I gained a special bond with my fellow Marines from those four years. That comes from the fact that you went through everything at the same time as a group; boot camp, training, combat drills. When that bond is developed, you know you can trust the person next to you.

That's the upside of it. The downside is the fact that barracks can be dry, meaning there is no alcohol allowed in the barracks. Period.

We're grown men and we were not allowed to have a glass of wine or a beer, even though half of the men had just come back from Afghanistan. The restrictions make you feel like you're back in pre-school, "Don't do this, don't do that," you're only allowed to eat during very specific time slots... unless you want to pay. "Be here at 1 am. If I call you at 2 am, be there." Those are aspects of life that civilians take for granted, without really understanding the shit that we're dealing with. But it all becomes worth it because seeing your best friend in the Marines have his first daughter, and being there for him, that's something you never forget. I found out about two of my buddies' first babies being born while I was on the range, but it was one of the proudest moments of my life because they're both very good friends of mine. Now I'm a proud uncle. These are the types of bonds that we build and nobody can ever take it from us.

As shitty as those four years were, I think the good still outweighs the bad. At the end of the day, nobody can tell me they have better job security. I'm going to keep getting paid unless I do something stupid like break the law.

*During your transition after you left the military, how did that go down?*

In my case, I didn't have a choice. I got injured and I had to have surgery, and I was on a nine-month waiting list. During that time, I was also getting pumped with medications like steroids and other narcotics. After surgery, I gained a lot of weight and was given six months to lose the weight. Unfortunately, I didn't lose the weight fast enough, so I was separated from the Marines which was a big blow. Right now, the Marines are trying to cut down from 200,000 to 187,000 so people are getting cut left and right for minor transgressions or things that would normally be waived. But by how things were going, I was kind of expecting how it was going to go down.

*Adonal Foyle, MA, MBA*

I know I mentioned that the good outweighs the bad, but that's more on a personal level. On a professional level, when you're 17 or 18 years old, or even 19 years old, you're still trying to figure out who you are as a man. Even now, I'm still trying to figure myself out. But as an 18-year-old, you're accustomed to being told what to do, where to go, and who to see. You go to school every day, you know you have to be home at a certain time, and you know you have a house to go home to. When you're in the military, the same thing is happening and you get accustomed to it. Now that I'm a bit older, I'm realizing that I want to pave my own way. I don't want to spend the rest of my life being told what to do and how to do it. Of course, you're not going to completely get away from being told to do things, but for me, I think it's one of the main reasons why I'm glad I got out of the military.

Looking at all my friends, they're 22- to 28-year-old men who have done a lot of things. They've seen the world. When it comes down to deciding whether or not we want to leave the military, or stay, one of the things we think about when it comes to staying is, "Do I know how to do anything else? Am I going to be good at anything else? Do I want to go back to college?" It's more about convenience when you're thinking about staying in the military. If you make a name for yourself in the community, there's no reason to leave.

Sometimes that's a good thing. But there are other people who say they can't deal with the fact that they're not allowed to have a glass of scotch unless they go somewhere downtown and spend money on it. You can't have a bottle of alcohol or a woman in your room because it's illegal. You can't have your girlfriend spend the night unless you plan to lose rank... things that sound silly when you're a grown ass man talking about what you can and can't do. If I want to see my girlfriend, I shouldn't have to give a shit what time of night it is. **When you were told you were done, what were your initial thoughts?**

I was pretending that I was happy, but the truth was, I was pissed. I was pissed because I felt fucked over. I was ordered to take medications because of my injury. There was no way I was able to get out of it. I was told that I had to do it. I didn't choose to get injured. I didn't want to have surgery. I didn't want to deal with the everyday pain. I didn't want to take any narcotics and be in a fog. I hate the idea of anything that alters my mind. But I had to do it. And maybe medicine caused me to get so pissed. My injury happened while I was in the Marine Corps; I didn't have any prior conditions. I'm not blaming it solely on the military—I know for a fact I could have eaten better.

I feel it's all too common that the people who are leaving aren't being taken care of anymore. Because now that the war is over, it's not about getting the mission done because there is no mission. We have small missions, but the overall joint unified effort is no longer there. Now, it's all about making your career progress and now there's just a whole bunch of buddy fucking, throwing people under the bus. I've watched that happen to so many people, including myself. I was livid. I was sad. I was hurt, and I was ashamed because I failed (or at least it felt like I failed).

## *What hurt, exactly?*

My pride, more than anything. Because I felt like I couldn't make it. For me, I had never failed at anything before in my life. And when I did, it hit me a lot harder than it would hit someone else who has dealt with failure in their life. I didn't just brush it off like a lot of people can. I really took it to heart. I really felt like I fucked up. And instead of correcting it, I got angry. I cried. I was angry at the world and I was angry at myself more than anything. I hated myself. I'd look in the mirror and say, "Who the fuck are you? You're nothing." When people were asking me if I was happy to get out, I would give them a fake smile, but at the end of the day, I would much rather be in the Marine Corps than where I am today.

My transition has been a lot harder than a lot of people think. People are generally happy to get out of the military. I went in the Marines expecting to be there for 20 years.

**Were you prepared emotionally to retire when you were forced to leave the military?**

Hell, no. I was not prepared emotionally or financially. I don't even want to think about all the money I blew. I was always a giving guy and people started to take advantage of that. At the end of the day, I didn't have any money for anything that *I* wanted.

Being released was the bitch slap I needed to get my shit together and move forward in life. The majority of my friends are still in the military and spread out across the country. And the reality is, of all those friends, I'm probably going to see one or two of them again in my life. I've been away from the military for a month and two days so maybe things will change.

**How do you feel now, compared to a month ago?**

Not much different. I still have anger problems. I take my anger out on people for things they don't deserve. For example, the feeling of failure is always in the back of my mind; the feeling that I wasn't good enough to stay. It's the little things that annoy me. Like when I'm driving on the freeway and someone honks at me because they want to go around. Most people would just be a little annoyed, but I become livid. I see what's wrong with other people and it reminds me of my own failures and it pisses me off.

*After leaving the military, what are the three biggest changes in your life?*

First, I had no guaranteed steady income. In the military, I knew I was going to get paid on the 1st and 15th of each month. I knew exactly how much it was going to be.

Second, it would be a guaranteed roof over my head. I'm lucky because I had housing waiting for me when I was out. But for a lot of people leaving the military, that's an issue.

Third, the hardest change for me is the way I act toward people and the way they act toward me. When you're in civilian life, nobody is in a rush. And for me, I've had a hard time getting accustomed to that. Everything seems so laid back, slow, and low key to me. I'm bored shitless half of the time because when I'm given a task to do, I finish it in an hour when it usually takes someone five hours. I'm wired to just go, go, go. And everything around me seems so slow. By the time it's 6 pm, I'm thinking, "Can I go to bed now?" because there's nothing left in the day to do.

There's also the aspect of how people talk to each other. I curse a lot more than the average person. It's just the environment I was accustomed to. When I talk to people, I'm pretty cut and dry, and to the point. When it's business, there's no room to ask, "How's it going? How's the wife and kids?" I don't give a shit. I couldn't care less because I'm looking for a job. When someone asks, "How was the military?" I want to say, "It was fine, now where's the computer because I have shit to do." When people smart off to me in a business environment, I'm about two seconds away from popping someone.

**What has helped you so far with your retirement? What type of coping skills have you acquired?**

Going to the gym. It gets a lot of testosterone out. I go to the gym every morning and get a lot of steam out. I have a personal trainer who tells me what to do. I don't really do a lot of lifting, it's more like doing tire flips and taking a sledgehammer and beating a tire with it. When I'm done at the gym, I'm exhausted and I like that feeling because that means my mind isn't dwelling on other things.

I also quit smoking cigarettes and chewing tobacco. Although those habits were calming to me, they were also bad habits. It reached a point where I couldn't even feel the buzz anymore. I'll smoke a cigar once every other day but these past three days, I've had a cigar every day, and that's the most I've smoked since I've been out. But now, I feel like it's not the end of the world if I don't smoke.

Talking to my girlfriend really helps because she's the only one who can really calm me down. Other people can say the exact same things that she does but it doesn't affect me the way it does when she says it. I know she loves me, and I love her. I know that speaking with her is just calming to me.

**What kind of support does the military provide in terms of transitioning out?**

We're given a week-long class called TRS (Transition Readiness Seminar). During the classes you have to wear proper civilian attire. They want you in slacks or khakis and a button-down polo shirt for a casual corporate environment. We only go by first names, instead of our last names. The VA comes to tell us about all the benefits we can get, and then the Department of Labor comes in and tells us about all the different ways we can find jobs. It's a week's worth of them trying to teach us how to be good civilians. It doesn't work because all they're doing is just lecturing us on how to be civilians again, and you can't lecture on how to be a civilian; it's more of a hands-on thing, we just have to walk through it.

Put me through workshops where I can be exposed to different situations to see how I deal with each situation. Put me in a job interview setting. Instead of showing me how to do VA stuff, take me to the VA center and show me what benefits I have personally. But I know that's not feasible because so many people are getting out right now. Damned if you do, damned if you don't. I did my TRS in July and I got out in October. Since then, I've forgotten everything they told me.

*Since you've been out, what resources have you been using?*

I've taken advantage of the disability clinic. I put the claim in before I left the military and I'm still waiting on a doctor's appointment to help verify, so they know I'm not just making it up. In the meantime, I can't do anything else.

I can also apply for a VA loan at really good prices. I'm not eligible for the GI Bill, but most people who normally get out of the military are eligible.

*What's next for you?*

I'm not 100% sure where my story will go from here. But there are options. I have something lined up with a local company. I'm working for a friend of mine. I'm doing whatever odd jobs there are. That's what's ultimately going to set me up in life. Because I'm willing to do just about anything to keep trucking.

**Update: November 2019**

It's been almost four years since my interview with Ryan. I caught up with him and asked what's been going on since he transitioned from the military.

I secured a job that I enjoy immensely; working with veterans, helping them receive their benefits and gain a better quality of life. I've surrounded myself with people who care about me and who help me strive to better myself and achieve great things. I'm not 100% where I want to be in life but I know I'm on the right path and I no longer doubt every aspect of what I know I'm capable of doing.

*Adonal Foyle, MA, MBA*

Transition is hard. I still struggle to find that perfect balance but all in all I've discovered that it's the people I choose to have around me and also engaging the right mindset that keeps me striving to succeed. I can say that every single day I'm constantly heading in the right direction toward what I want and how I want my life to look.

## Alexus Foyle
Retired, Semi-Pro Basketball Player
Active 2006-2014

*Tell me about your basketball career.*

I played semi-pro overseas. And it was different over there because in the U.S., you're allowed to create your own shots. But when I played in Taiwan, I was scoring a lot of points, but my coach practically said I needed to create shots for my teammates. So I needed to play more team-oriented basketball. I had to pass first, then create a shot for myself, yet I needed to keep my teammates involved. In college, I drew a lot of attention from the opposing teams to free up the rest of my teammates. So playing that kind of basketball was hard in a sense, but it took me back to college. That was the main difference. It wasn't just about me scoring anymore. It was about involving everybody.

*When did you start thinking about hanging it up?*

Two years ago. I had a job in Taiwan and I was making pretty good money. Then, I was given joke jobs to go to Venezuela for way less money—money I couldn't survive on. It got to the point where I was facing an uphill battle trying to make money to play basketball. I started to realize that I needed to start making the transition out of basketball, and it was pretty, pretty tough.

*What was your transition like?*
It was pretty tough. I still have my moments because I still feel like I can play at a high level. So it was really, really tough for me to hang it up and tell myself that I had to stop playing. I felt like I had a lot left in my tank, and also felt like I didn't get my full value out of playing

basketball. I was always underpaid and I wanted to keep on going to reach that high level. But at the same time, I was getting older, and once I started watching my age, I realized I wasn't going to get a proper job in basketball, I said to myself, "Shit, I have to let it go." So it's hard. I still have my moments every time I play ball.

Whenever we're playing pickup games, people ask me why I stopped playing professionally because they knew I could still play. And I knew I could still play, but there was no money in it anymore, but I also knew that I needed to survive, and that's tough. Right now, at my regular job, I still have those thoughts of, "Shit, I need to be playing basketball." But I'm making good money at my job right now, so it's okay. I'm now at a job where I work 20 days and I get 10 days off per month so that part made the transition a little easier.

**Looking back at your last two years of retirement, what has been the most difficult thing about walking away from the sport?**

Knowing that I was no longer going to be playing basketball at that high competitive level. From here on out, I will only be playing for recreation. I may still play against a bunch of pros, but it will only be in an open-gym situation.

**What do you most miss about playing basketball?**

The cohesiveness. The coaches. There were some guys I didn't like, but for the most part I got along with everyone. I also miss the traveling and going to different cities, being on the bus, and just playing. I miss talking to my teammates and having fun. Because I knew my teammates had my back. At my regular job, I still work with co-workers and we're still a team but it's not the same as being on a team in basketball. I was born to play basketball. I know it.

*Was your retirement voluntary or involuntary (due to injuries, diminished skills, age, etc.)?*

My retirement was involuntary. It was age. I had to retire because of my age.

*At the time, were you ready to retire?*

No.

*How did you prepare yourself for retirement?*

I didn't prepare. It was one of those things where I couldn't get a job, I couldn't survive on the money I was being offered, and I had to think about what the next step was. I didn't have any money saved up so I just kept stringing along.

*What thoughts did you have about retirement before you retired?*

To tell you the truth, I thought I was going to play basketball forever. I never thought I would have to retire. I knew in the back of my mind I would at some point because of Father Time, but I really did think I would be playing forever.

*What does a bad day look like for you when you're thinking about basketball after retirement?*

A bad day is when one of my coaches calls me while I'm at work and says there's a game going on at the gym and Kevin Durant is going to be there. They're asking for me to come and I can't be there. That's a bad day for me. Sometimes I'll play at Rucker Park (in New York) with the pros and they'll tell me that I should start a league. To hear NBA players comment on my game like that is great. But at the same time, I start thinking about how I need to be at that level. And I can't. That just breaks me down. But playing pro ball overseas, I was fine with it because I still got to play basketball. And now I'm done at that level. And again, I can still play open gym. That gets me going.

**Looking back at your career, what would you tell your son about the game of basketball based on what you learned?**

Don't expect anything to be given to you. It's a dog-eat-dog world in basketball. It's all about who you know, not what you know. I would also have my son work on every aspect of his game. That way, he has no weakness. For me, when I played, I didn't play high school basketball, so I knew my game had some weaknesses. I know I could have overcome that and played in the NBA, but they used my weaknesses to keep me back. I didn't have a legitimate argument because they were right. So I would tell my son to: a) take care of your grades in school, b) work your ass off and make sure you are great at what you do. If you can do that, you can leave everything else to God.

**When you look back at the last two years, what helped you get through your retirement?**

One thing that helped me even before I played basketball was I always had a job. When I was still living on the islands, I was always working so it was easy for me to grab a job when I was done playing basketball. If I wasn't always working on the islands, the transition from basketball to work would have been tougher. I worked before basketball and now I'm working after basketball so for me, basketball was just something in the middle.

One of the things that also helped me with my transition are the people that I love and care for, like my mom. I always wanted to help her if she needed something. So I never thought about myself; I thought about the people I cared about. I always tried not to be selfish.

*What were the three biggest changes you experienced after you stopped playing?*

I now go to work every day at an 8-to-14 hour job. It's tough because I'm now working in an oil field and I'm dealing with explosives. But working long days, I sometimes feel like falling asleep. Waking up at 6 in the morning, driving to work, working 14 hours, and then driving back while trying not to fall asleep at the wheel.

*What is your job at the oil field?*

There are riggers, frackers and wire lines. I'm at the wire line and I work with the frackers. We go down, set up explosives and create holes underground that are two feet wide where the oil starts to come out. So my job is pretty dangerous. Before we go on location, my stress level is at zero. But when we head down to start fracking, my stress level shoots way up because it's so intense. You walk around with pipes in your hand, and if a pipe explodes, it can cut you. It's also a nice penny so that eases the stress a little bit.

*What do you miss most about playing basketball?*

I miss dunking on people. I had one dunk that stood out. There was a dude who stood 6-foot-11. I went baseline and bypassed the rim. He jumped and tried to block me, but the rim barred him. And I dunked on him so hard face-to-face. He was running behind me because I passed him. I turned around to dunk and I posterized him in the head. This happened in Queens, NY and I was told it was the No. 1 dunk in the city. That's one dunk that really stands out. That's when I felt like I was really meant to play basketball.

*Adonal Foyle, MA, MBA*

**Looking at your past two years, what are your thoughts on retirement so far?**

It's great. I'm now making more money than when I was playing. Once you make more money, it takes a lot of the pressure off. Of course, money is not all happiness. I still want to play the game, but I'm now at a job where my work gives me flexibility where I can still play basketball for fun. I have the best of both worlds because I can still play basketball and I can still make money. Plus, I have 10 days off per month, and that's 10 days to play basketball.

**How did your relationships with family and friends change after your retirement?**

They probably became better. When I was playing, I was out of the country. When I was playing in Taiwan, it was crazy and I didn't have a lot of time to talk to them. Now, I can go home more often to see the family. And now that I'm back in America, I can talk to them even more. So I'm actually a lot closer to my family than when I was playing.

**Who is Alexus Foyle today?**

I'm a coach. I go to the gym, I see kids, and I'll work with the ones who really want to learn the game. I'll shoot with them and teach them the fundamentals.

**If you had to do it all over again, what would you do differently?**

One thing I would do differently is I would try to learn the game at the elementary level. Then, I would definitely work on all aspects of my game. I would have been a better ball handler. On the islands, I didn't know any better. I had nobody to teach me down there. So if I had to do it all over again, I would just make sure my shot is right so I could figure out what position best suits me. I don't really blame myself for how I learned to play basketball because I was a late bloomer.

***Did anyone within the sport help you with your transition?***

Nobody really told me anything about retirement. One thing I tried to do while learning the game was talk to you, and try to take a page out of your book, and watch what I was doing. You were always a huge support for me. I reached far in basketball because I looked up to you. But when it came to retirement, nobody even talked to me. There wasn't ever a discussion. It was more about going to work and making something happen.

*Adonal Foyle, MA, MBA*

## Roy Byrd, Sr.
**Vietnam War Veteran , US Army**
**(Active Duty 1966-1985)**
**(1945-2020)**

*Talk about your experiences being in the Vietnam War.*

I don't think anyone knew what it was going to be like to go over there. When I went, I was 19 years old and I stayed there for a year. When you're there, you just have to make the best of it. You try to understand why you're there in the first place, and you try to learn as much as you can. As soldiers, we were already trained before getting to Vietnam. But when you get there, and get down to it, it's totally different.

When you're in combat, you do what you have to do, but when you go home and there are so many anti-war people who don't like you or have their own perceptions of the war, you have to carry on as much as possible. For me, nobody made me go to war and nobody made me stay at war. Being in the military felt like a job, and I stayed in the military because it felt like a job. While still in the military, I got married and had kids, but eventually we divorced. I got married again and had another child, but things didn't work out. I think my issue was I tried really hard to stay at my military "job" so I could provide for my family. I didn't really think about the ups and downs that would come along with working and being a husband and father.

When I eventually got out of the military, I really had to think about what I wanted to do. I asked myself, "What now?" I tried to think about all the things I could do, but I didn't have too many people there for me to help me find the right job. I tried a lot of different jobs, but eventually I got a call from the post office and they offered me a position paying $10 an hour; I worked there for 20 years.

For 10 of those 20 years, I had bad credit. I had a GI Bill but nobody wanted to talk to me because I didn't have a lot of money and I didn't have good credit.

When GIs come out of the military with nothing, they have to start somewhere, and most often that *somewhere* is starting from scratch. You're thinking, "Man, what am I going to do?" I saw a lot of GIs before I retired (with higher ranking than I had), and a lot of them were black and the military was forcing them out. These guys had kids, families, and the military was telling them, "We don't want you anymore." They told me that it was going to happen to me in four to five years but I paid no mind. I kept going.

The next thing I knew, I wound up in a hospital; I don't know how I got there because I didn't take drugs. All I remember was that I was supposed to go to Korea, and now I'm at this hospital. There was some talk of Agent Orange being involved but I didn't know what was going on, I didn't know who authorized using Agent Orange, and now I'm concerned about my wellbeing because I have kids to think about. I remember thinking, "What about my kids? What about my kids' kids?" All of a sudden, I'm told I need to retire because I have psychosis. I didn't even know what psychosis was. I asked the doctor what it was and he just told me to look it up in the dictionary.

I think about all the soldiers since the 1960s who got out of the military. I wonder what happened to them. The military isn't telling them anything, and they have a lot of health problems. For me, I'm a diabetic. I shoot insulin every night. There are still some people in the military fighting for their benefits.

### *Did the military ever examine you for Agent Orange?*

No. I don't think they even know what it is. Whenever the topic of Agent Orange comes up, nobody likes to talk about it.

*Adonal Foyle, MA, MBA*

**Talk about getting out of the military. What was it like for you?**

We caught a lot of heat from everyone when we came back. I had to pull that uniform off to avoid hostility from so much of the public. The post office was the first to really give me a chance. When you apply for the post office, they give you a test; you start with 10 points and you need to score at least a 90 to get hired. So they hired me. I didn't do much else except go to work. I had four years to use my GI Bill but I never used it so I lost it.

**Talk about the experience of being hated by the public for participating in the Vietnam War.**

It made me feel bad. When I came home from Vietnam, I used to go to Downtown Oakland with my uniform on. One person yelled at me, "You're a baby killer!" I thought, "No, I'm not a baby killer." People took pictures of me, others told me I wasn't welcome in the area. I always wondered, "Why is everyone so pissed at us?" I didn't stop to think about it. I went to Fort Benning in Georgia, and the same thing happened over there. Everyone was so pissed off. But what people didn't understand was that nobody liked this country. Even in Germany, we got heat. I felt bad, but I couldn't sit around and feel sorry for myself. I went looking for jobs. Some people would be nice and talk to me but others weren't so nice. All you can do is wash it off. Now, it's a lot better.

**What were some of the difficulties you experienced in being a civilian again?**

It took me a while to adjust my mindset. I've been through a lot, including two divorces. I went to see the kids as much as I could. I was constantly looking for jobs. I felt that I was done wrong because if I was leaving the military with only 30% of my pay, somebody is not telling me something. There's still a lot of stuff going on in the military...and they're never going to tell us what happened to us.

*Winning the Transition Game*

***What unit did you serve with in Vietnam and talk about your experiences there?***

I was an infantry guy. We were always in the field. We would stay at basecamp for about two or three days a month, but the rest of the time, we were in the field. And if we ran into anything going on, we were in the field a lot longer. It was similar to what people went through in Iraq but instead of the desert we were in the jungle. We had to avoid the three or four miles of roads leading to the main highway because there were minesweepers. When I first got to Vietnam, my unit was already in the field so they flew me over there in a helicopter. By the time I met up with my unit, they were already searching and destroying. I did not see a basecamp for the first 30 days.

We would get into a skirmish with the enemy and they would run. Sometimes guys got hurt through combat or booby traps. It sunk in —those Viet Cong guys ain't playing. I learned how to set booby traps because I was determined that I wasn't going to die there. We were a search and destroy unit; we searched everywhere to see where the enemy was. We'd stay in one area for a week, just looking around. We were all around 19 years old.

All in all, we lost about seven soldiers in our unit. One of them, I knew. His name was Parker and he was from Augusta, Georgia. We were walking down the road one day and all of a sudden we decided to walk off to the side. We figured we were going to go through the jungle instead of the roads. I was an RTO (Radio Transmit Operator). Parker was the last guy in our platoon. We walked around one of the mines, but Parker didn't. He stepped on it. We heard an explosion and we turned around. I saw Parker flying in the air and everyone else got down. The enemy knew we were there. I sat in the bushes, crying. The other platoon guys asked me if I was okay. "No!" I replied. Earlier in the day, we had not seen one Vietnamese person but once the mine went off, they were all over the place. That night, I couldn't sleep. I just sat there thinking about how I could get out of there. Eventually, I got used to staying out in the field. The more you chased the enemy, the better off you were. If you were stuck at basecamp, you got bored.

*Adonal Foyle, MA, MBA*

***When you came home and were trying to figure out how to move on with your life, what things made your transition work?***

Being in Vietnam, and being in fights, you learn. Sometimes the Viet Cong would shoot at us and then they would run. While you're in Vietnam, you have to take care of yourself. Once I got out, I thought constantly about everything I went through over there. I talked to some of the guys at the post office about my experiences because many of them had been involved with wars. We'd all sit and talk about everything we'd been through.

***Looking back, what is the most difficult thing for you to handle now, having gone through diabetes, divorces, etc.?***

For me, the most difficult thing is dealing with Agent Orange, although money is also a problem. I can't go to the VA and ask for more money. Some people still try to fight the military for more money but it doesn't work. When you get out of the military, you have to approach it knowing that you need to start somewhere, and the truth is, some guys don't want to start somewhere. They're stuck thinking the military still owes them something. But the military owes you nothing. You go in, you get out, and that's it.

***How did you deal with racism while in the military, and how did you deal with it when you got out?***

When I got out, I dealt with the Black Panthers, who not only didn't believe in war, but also considered me a sellout for being a soldier. I understood what they were doing for black people and I can't hate them for that. I just went on. When I got out of the military, Oakland didn't seem like Oakland to me anymore. But then I was told that when you get out of the military, you get jet lagged in the head because of what you were so used to seeing when you were fighting. You have to set your mind to it that it's just a job. That's what it was for me. The military was just a job. But when I got out, I had nobody.

*How did your family handle your divorce?*

At times, the kids were mad. But there were times when they were mad at their mom, too. I wanted them to know that their mom didn't do anything wrong. I messed the marriage up. I gave her the choice to stay with me or to leave. She made the decision to leave, but it was because of me messing it up. I told them if they wanted to hate someone, they should hate me, and also if they couldn't visit their mom and conduct themselves the way they should, then they shouldn't visit her.

One time, Roy and I were nose to nose with each other. I didn't hate him for it. I loved him for it because he allowed his frustration to come out. He let it all out on how the divorce was affecting him. I wanted my kids to know I was going to help them out as much as I could; I'm always going to be their father. I hate that I wasn't there all the time, but I appreciated them whenever they asked me to hang out with them. They saw me as someone who was working all the time at the post office, so they probably didn't want to bother me. Vietnam really taught me a lot of things. Whenever I was frustrated, I learned how to back off. I learned how to chill out. A lot of people can't do that.

*What does happiness mean to you now?*

I'm glad that I'm still alive and that I'm doing my best to take care of myself and my kids and grandkids. There's nothing else I can do about the things that have happened to me so I just try to live my life the best way I can every day. I'm not getting any younger. I'm 69 now.

*What could the military have done differently for you and other soldiers?*

The military should have discussions with people who are about to join. They should go back to the draft. That's just what I believe. If the draft came back, kids would come out of high school and join the military for two years. Kids are graduating high school without a job or a plan, but if they join the military, they get to eat three times a day. They would receive training. And if they made good on their test scores, a job will be waiting for them. If a soldier wants to stay in the military, he or she can always re-enlist. These days, there are kids with nothing to do, nowhere to go, and they sometimes join gangs. If you're in the military, you don't have time to be bored.

*If you had to do it all over again, what would you do differently?*

Nothing. Because the government doesn't owe us anything.

ಸಂ ಲ

Since the writing of this book, Staff Sergeant Roy Byrd Sr. has passed away due to complications from his exposure to Agent Orange during his service in the Vietnam War. A 26-year Infantry Veteran with the United States Army, Roy served his Country faithfully and with dedication. Following his Military service, he continued to dedicate his life to his Country and community, working at the United States Postal Service for 20 years. In addition to his time with Federal Service he worked as Security Personnel for the Oakland Athletics, spending majority of his time beloved by the season ticket holders of the left Field bleachers.

Staff Sergeant Roy Byrd Senior passes away on August 21st, survived by his two daughters, his 3 sons, and his 9 grandchildren. He will be loved and missed by all those that came in contact with him.

# Mark Munoz
Retired Mixed Martial Artist (UFC)
Active 2007-2015 in MMA

*Having won national titles and becoming a two-time All-American, what inspired you to switch from wrestling to MMA?*

I've always believed that you're a product of your environment. I had been wrestling since I was in the eighth grade. I never thought I'd be punching and kicking people in the face for a living. I never thought I'd do that because anyone who knows me knows that I'm a kind person. I want to give you a big hug and encourage you. I never want to beat someone up. My natural inclination is to want to comfort people. I never thought I'd punch and kick people in the face for a living, but I met a lot of people. I wrestled at Oklahoma State and I got beat up a lot. That kind of invoked a spirit within me. I was at Oklahoma State for a total of eight years (I wrestled there for five years and I coached there for three). Then I moved to UC Davis, where I was coaching the wrestling team there. I met a guy named Uriah Faber. In UFC he's known as The California Kid. He's a short, stocky dude. Long-blond hair and buff. He coached with me at UC Davis. When I was trying out for the Olympic team, Uriah would train with me. While I was training, Uriah got involved in MMA. He started telling me how much he loved it and thought I should get involved. At the time, I was coaching and I was teaching, I have a wife and three kids (with one on the way). I was thinking 'I don't have time to do MMA.' Uriah convinced me to just tell my wife that I was going to be good at it and I could make a lot of money.

One day, Uriah brought in some heavy hitters: Randy Couture and Quentin "Rampage" Jackson and Tito Ortiz, Brandon Vera—the 'who's who' of the UFC at the time. They were coming to Sacramento to do a training camp and Randy Couture had a fight to defend his title. I wanted to go watch it and they invited me to their practice. I was ready to watch everyone spar, but there were an off number of guys in the room. Everyone's partnering up and one guy was by himself – Randy Couture. I couldn't wait to see who was going to step in the octagon with him. At the same time, Uriah gave me a pair of gloves and headgear and asked if I could spar with Randy. I started to freak out, but Uriah said, "You'll be fine." The headgear was so big, I couldn't even see through it. And the gloves were really small and could barely cover my knuckles.

I got into the cage; Randy starts shadow boxing. Meanwhile I'm just doing stretches, not sure what I'm supposed to be doing. So they closed the cage door and locked it in. Now, it's real. The bell rings and now it's time to go. I see Randy coming in, bobbing his head and throwing jabs. I started swinging for the fences. I started swinging so hard, he was like 'whoa'... and I missed. He took me down and started to 'ground and pound' me. I reversed him and now I was on top of him. I hear Uriah yell 'ground and pound' and I start throwing down punches at his head. Randy was like 'Hey, we don't try to knock each other out in practice.' I thought we were supposed to do it. After we were scrambling in the cage, Randy takes off his head gear and says 'Hey Munoz, you really need to consider doing this.' I was like 'Really?' Then, Uriah slaps me across the chest and yells 'See? Told you, bro!' And that's how I got into it. Ten months later, I was in UFC.

**When you look back at your career, what would you say were the biggest highlights? And what did you love about the sport overall?**

What I loved about MMA and the UFC is that it connected a lot of people together. When I say that, whenever I was getting ready to fight, people would come out of the woodwork and support me. My coaches, my family and friends that I haven't seen in a long time. So my fights would bring everyone together. And after the fight, I would see all these people and all these emotions would run through my mind when I saw people I hadn't seen in a long time. We would reminisce, tell old stories about back in the days when we had fun times, played games, even when I had some adversity. I just loved the fact that it brought people together.

I also loved the camaraderie that MMA had within our team. There's a bond that you share with your fellow fighters that's unparalleled. I just loved that aspect.

***When it came to being successful during your career, what stood out to you?***

My career was up and down. I was ranked in the Top 3 in the last three years in my career, but it was up and down. I had some big losses; I had some great wins. At one point, I was a No. 1 contender. So for me, it was that up and down ride that made me realize that's how life is going to be. In real life, you're going to have some great victories. But you're also going to have some failure that you're going to have to rise above. So those were the things I had to learn. Because athletics and life are one and the same. You're going to have some wins and you're going to have some losses. But those losses are going to catapult you to winning the game or winning the match some way somehow. So when I look back, I'm thankful for having the career that I had. At the same time, I got out because I wanted to be with my family more often. I wasn't around a lot when I was fighting. I was traveling the world while my wife and four kids were at home. Then, my son wanted me to coach him in wrestling. My daughter wants me to be here for her. My two youngest kids are growing up fast. Now, I'm wondering 'Where's the time going?' So when I look back at my career, I can see how it parallels life. I love that aspect of it.

***Toward the end of your career, you were dealing with a lot of injuries. During that time, when did you have the first inclination where you thought maybe the end might be near?***

Throughout my whole career, I had been dealing with injuries. I broke little bones here and there. I have scars everywhere. And scars tell the story. Toward the end of my career, I cut a lot of weight. The most I ever lost in a fight was 75 pounds in 12 weeks. But my career has always been like that—the ups and downs in weight, even when I was wrestling in high school. I would weigh 225 to 245 pounds and I would cut it down to 180. Sometimes I would get a six-week notice that I need to cut down on weight. So I would go through these ups and downs. Because of that, my body started taking a toll. To this day, I still feel like my body is taking a toll from that.

I remember one time I made weight and my back was sore. So I was asking my coaches if they could massage my back. It felt tight. They told me that it wasn't my back that was bothering me... it was my kidneys. So I was rehydrating as much as I could. I didn't go to the bathroom for four days and my body started to get swollen because it was just holding on to the liquid. So I would press my skin and there would be a half-inch indention in my skin. I also had a herniated disk in my back. So I was dealing with a lot of different things. But what really had me thinking about retiring was the fact that I was traveling the world with UFC for eight years. I would be away from home for about a month, then I'd be home for a week, then go back on the road and be gone for a few more weeks. I was just never home.

So my son, who was a very good soccer and baseball player, went to the Little League World Series and did very well there. He also wrestled. He went to a wrestling tournament in Las Vegas and didn't win a match. I told him not to be so hard on himself because he was so focused on soccer and baseball that he hardly had time to practice wrestling. One day, my son told me that he wanted to quit soccer and baseball and focus on wrestling. I asked him why. He was so good at soccer and baseball and I just asked him why he would want to quit those sports to take up wrestling. He said he loved wrestling and he has a passion for it. I told him that he would have to cut weight, he might get hurt a lot. He didn't have to worry about that stuff in soccer and baseball. But he was committed to wrestling. So I started to ask him what his goals were. He wanted a full-ride scholarship to a Division I university. At this time, he's in the eighth grade. I started asking him 'Why are you thinking about this now?' Right now, there are 72 Division I colleges that offer full-ride scholarships in wrestling. There are tens of thousands of kids who want that scholarship. I asked him 'What makes you think that out of the tens of thousands of kids who want a full-ride scholarship to a Division I school, that you'll be able to get one?' Without batting an eye, he looks at me and says 'I got you, Dad.'

That hit me in the chest so hard. That was the straw that broke the camel's back. That's when I decided I was done. So six weeks before my last fight, I announced that I was going to retire. I wanted to be there for my family. I was sitting back and watching my wife be a superwoman. She was shuttling the kids here and there, taking care of the house. And she was running my gym. I'm sure it was crazy for her. So I knew it was time. I could take care of these injuries. But time was fleeting. I can't get time back. At the time, I had a daughter who was going to leave the house in two years.

Fast forward to four years later, my son now has that full-ride scholarship, my daughter is in college, and my two younger kids are on their way to doing the same thing. Now, looking back, I could see the benefits of me retiring because I see my family benefitting from it.

***Once you made the announcement that you were going to retire, did anything cross your mind leading up to that final fight?***

Yes! At the time, I was this close to getting a world title fight... and I could win. At the time, the champion was Michael Bisping. He was training at my gym and I did really well against him. At this time, I'm thinking 'I can be the champ.' There was a little part of me that felt like I needed to keep going. But I also started to think 'What's the most important thing?' So I had to snap back and stay focused on what I wanted to do. In my mind, I knew that I could still do it. But I don't regret the decision that I made. I see where my family is now, and I wouldn't change it for the world.

**What would you say was the most difficult part of retirement, in terms of transitioning to another career?**

The most difficult part was that I was making a large bulk of my income by fighting. And now that was gone. But in addition to that, the exhilaration of competing and climbing the ranks, and doing it in front of a large crowd. I was doing that 5-6 times a year. Not having that anymore was big to me. So you could call it a mid-life crisis. That was hard to deal with because now I had to transition into something that will help provide for my family for the long term.

Today, I'm coaching. What I'm doing now is helping others get to the level where I once was. My goal now is to get them to be the best fighters that they can be, whether it's on the wrestling mat or inside the octagon. I also coach my son and I own a gym. Who knows? There may be a fighter coming out of my gym who will be the next UFC star. I still do work for the UFC. I just came back from a tour in Iraq and Kuwait. Before that, I went to Japan and Guam. During these tours, I teach our troops how to do hand-to-hand combat. I love doing all of these things. At the same time, it took me a while to transition. And it was hard.

**Is there anything you would have done differently?**

Hindsight is 20/20. So yes, there are some things I would have done differently looking back. When I signed with UFC, I was coaching with Uriah in Northern California. Then, I moved to Southern California and opened my own gym, Reign Training. So that whole time, I had my hand in a lot of things.

Having said that, I wasn't a fighter first. Having said all that, I would have done a lot of that differently. If I had the gym, I would have withdrawn a little more so I could focus more on myself, then worry about everyone else later. While I was traveling as a fighter, I was also traveling as a coach. I would go with other fighters and wrestlers and be their cornerman. I would coach kids on the weekends and try to make every family event I could get to. At the same time, I was trying to be an elite mixed martial artist and compete at the professional level. I was trying to do everything, and I couldn't do them perfectly. So something had to give. And that's when my body started breaking down. I didn't get the ample rest and recovery that I needed. Then I needed surgery here, surgery there. I had a herniated disk. So I was putting a lot of miles into my body at the time.

***If you had a fellow fighter approach you today, telling you that he or she was contemplating retirement, what would you tell that person?***

If they're thinking about retiring, I would tell them that they need to have a plan. They need an action plan for retirement. What are you going to do to replace the income you were making as a professional fighter? More importantly, what are you going to do to replace the routine you used to have, practicing every day and competing against the top fighters in the world? That's first and foremost. So you need to have an action plan for your time and your money. The most important thing is to find a way to make use of the time you're going to have. And obviously, you have to think of how you will generate income because you have to provide for your family.

Then, they need to have the mental strength to be able to talk about transition while they're retired. When you're used to the lights and interviews, autographs and people wanting to take pictures with you, you can get caught up in that stuff. When you don't have that anymore, you almost lose your identity. So I would ask that person: 'Where do you place your identity? Are you a UFC fighter? Or are you a husband, father, friend or business owner... who happens to be a UFC fighter?' Is that identity someone who is in it for the long haul? So I would tell that person to place that identity in something that lasts, not something that's futile.

**How did the UFC help you with your transition? And do you think they have to have a better way to help fighters such as yourself?**

I strongly agree that the UFC has to do more for the fighters. We go out there, we train, we compete, we put our bodies on the line. Sometimes, some guys suffer long-term effects as a result. Right now, we don't have pensions. We don't have retirement benefits. We don't have medical. We don't have any of that stuff. When we're done competing, we don't have anything. So now we have to figure out what we can do with the things we have garnered through the years we competed. Some guys retire without much clout. So they have to scrounge what they have. Or sometimes they go and work at a regular job, which is fine too. It just depends on what they can do. But I feel that the UFC can do a better job in supporting those who have competed in their organization.

I think the UFC can also hold summits and educate people on retirement a little bit more and teach them how they can transition into different things. Maybe have different jobs for people who retire.

# Sharon Ann Cohen
**Retired Sr. VP in the insurance marketing field**

*TURN! TURN! TURN!*

*To everything there is a season,
and a time for every purpose under heaven;
A time to be born, and a time to die;
a time to plant, and a time to reap that which is planted.*

**Performed by The Byrds, 1965
Song writer: Pete Seeger, late 1950s
Origin: Ecclesiastes 3:1 3:2, late 3rd century, BC**

Briefly, I worked 34 years in the insurance marketing field. The last 23 with Aon, a brokerage company, rising from a marketing manager to a senior vice president, leading a team of 40 creative folks. We crafted strategy, built plans, created campaigns, managed events and excelled at managing people and making things happen. Some of my time was working in the global arena, with about 20% of the time traveling. Visited a lot of exotic places and made good friends along the way. Loved my life, was challenged by the work and had lots of energy for being a working mom and wife. My heart and soul always remained at home with Rick and Alex (he was 12 at the time of my travel). On top of that, I was fortunate to have a big, extended family in the neighborhood and dear friends, all within minutes of my home.

Fast forward to 2009 and after, when we had lost four parents, all of whom were sick for a while; a granddaughter; celebrated Alex and Cynthia's wedding; overcame health issues; struggled with ever-changing technology and survived the recession.

So, it was time for me to look around and see that the joy of living was simply being sucked out of me. I was feeling overwhelmed, dragging myself to work, out of shape, heavy and unhappy... not my natural state. The treadmill of life was wearing me out. Retirement beckoned.

I read a lot of books on retirement, how to follow your passion, etc. but none of them spoke to me like Younger Next Year for Women, by Chris Crowley and Henry S. Lodge, M.D. So I transitioned all the successful work habits into working at being in motion six days a week for the rest of my life... and I feel wonderful.

So what else is different? The company will flourish with another marketing leader. My work friends are still available for a visit. There are friends from Book Group, long-time girlfriends, sisters, who have all connected more now that our years of kids in the house are over. We all know the Wife/Mom/Grandmother roles can trump all other activities. I listen better and take more time to consider other opinions. I enjoy my day more. I say "Yes" to new options without thinking about how I can add one more thing to my day. I daydream and sleep better. Time with my granddaughter is the whipped cream and cherries of life. With her, I rediscovered play and discovery. My garden is beautiful. We eat at home more often, with healthier meals. We entertain more. I sit on a non-profit board, the League of Women Voters, which increases my political understanding and engagement. I enjoy the new, diverse, daily workout and meeting new people at the Y. Our marriage is flourishing. The Florida Panhandle, with Southern hospitality and Emerald Green waters lapping white beaches, has been an absolute joy for Rick and me. And finally, we only have to negotiate one work schedule when we want to take a vacation.

The downside? I am no longer a United Mileage Plus airline boarder, more careful with spending, and feeling my time is less valuable. What a small insignificant list.

I am grateful, beyond measure, for my day-by-day life.

## Mark Blount

Nine-year NBA veteran. Mark was a center with four teams in the National Basketball Association Active 2000-2007.

*What was it like to play in the NBA, then eventually transition out of the league into another career?*

Playing in the league was a dream come true. While you're there, you're living like a rock star. Everything is catered to you and anything is available for you. That's one of the things that players, in my opinion, have a problem with when they retire because while the league does everything for you while you're playing, after you're done playing, the league is done with you. You're on your own. Most players have difficulty adjusting their mindset in the transition period.

*Talk about that first day you walked away from the league. Did you have a plan on what you wanted to do next?*

No. I had no plan at all. I just stayed at home, writing things down. I had a lot of ideas, but I eventually tore them all up because they were all bad ideas. So I packed four suitcases, flew out to London and ended up living there for a year.

*What did you learn while you were in London?*

I just spent time learning about the world and different cultures. I spent a lot of time being around people of all ages, younger or older. I was seeking out wisdom because despite living a good life in the U.S., there's a whole different world out there. There are a lot of different cultures and there are still a lot of good people left in this world. I now have friends all over the world.

*Adonal Foyle, MA, MBA*

*Before you left the league, what were your thoughts on taking that first step?*

What I initially thought, and what actually happened, became two different things. I did a lot of thinking, but the most important thing to me came from (Boston Celtics owner) Wyc Grousbeck. He said if I was going to start a business, I had to make sure I was there every day. So getting that wisdom from someone like him made me realize that I can't do anything productive if I can't be there every day to watch the money. That's why I went to London to figure it out and learn about myself and think about what I wanted to do next.

**If you could go back and say something to your former self when he's on the verge of retiring, what would you say to yourself?**

I would definitely tell him to be a little more patient. You can understand what you want to do, but you also have to completely understand the process. If you want to run four restaurants at the same time, make sure you know how to do something like that and deal with employees, payroll and things like that. You can't run your business the way your coach used to yell at you. On the real estate side, I would tell my former self that maybe he should learn how to use a screwdriver and put up 2x4s, which I had a crash course in doing because I had to do it all by myself. If you buy something that was made in 1962, and it still looks like it's from 1962, you can't make money off that. So my friend and I renovated everything, and that's how I learned about construction and how to use tools like saws and drills. I would have never learned any of that stuff if I didn't start my own company and be able to make money.

**How long did it take for you to realize that there was a path ahead of you toward that transition?**

After living in London for a year, I had a better understanding of what I wanted to do. I was able to reach out to one of my mentors—Charles Smith, another former NBA player—and he talked to me about some of the things he's been through and all the bad decisions he made. When you have a chance to speak with a fellow NBA player, who played a generation ahead of you, I was able to take some pointers from him and add some things that other players have done and figure out what worked best for me.

***When it came to the league preparing players for transitioning out of their playing career, how did they help you?***

When I was in the league, I thought they were fair. But they need to get more current players involved so they can have people who can relate to what players are going through and talk to them about some of the things they're thinking about when it comes to retirement and transition. Charles Smith told me that the first thing I needed to do was find a great business lawyer. Little things like that that came from a fellow NBA player goes a long way.

***If you were to talk to a current player today, who's thinking about retiring, what advice would you give him and what would you say he can expect as he leaves the game?***

I would tell him to be patient and take his time. There's no rush trying to catch up with Warren Buffett. Understand what you want to do. Because whatever it is, you have to have a passion for what you want to do next. You have to want to wake up every day to do it. If you're doing it just for the money, I don't know if it's going to work out well for you. For me, learning to run restaurants, learning to do real estate and learning to do renovation work was a passion for me. So I didn't have a problem answering phone calls and having to go fix things.

*Adonal Foyle, MA, MBA*

**When it comes to saving your money, how important is that for someone who wants to take his time thinking about what he wants to do next, and using resources to learn about whatever that next career is going to be?**

It's very important because you still have a family, you still have a life to live. During that process, it could just take one year. For others, it could be 3-4 years. So you definitely need to save your funds in order to take the time to think about what you want to do next.

**How important was education for you, in terms of giving you a good foundation for what you wanted to do next?**

Education was definitely a must for me. Not only the education part but being at a university with friends who have very good positions that I can actually call now. People I can work with and get information from. So education was not only very important but having friendships while at my university.

**When you transitioned out of the league, how did it affect you mentally?**

For me, the mental side will never go away. It was more about subduing my ego. If someone asked me for advice about how to handle it mentally, I would just tell them to go about it day by day and go from there. Because at one point, we were one of the top basketball players in the world, playing in the best league. A lot of us were lucky to make pensions and do a lot of good things for our families. But the ego is always in us, because we needed it to get us in the league to begin with. That fire is always burning. And that goes back to the patience I was talking about. We always want it and we always want to go get it. It's a mental fight every day. It was bad for me for those first 3-4 years of retirement.

# Conclusion

# Rediscovering Your Inner Athlete

> *"In the space between chaos and shape there was another chance."*
>
> **Jeanette Winterson**

For many people retirement is like the death of a passion, while for others, it is a welcome change of course. Each person's journey is unique with its own peaks and valleys. Some mornings you get up and the world seems like an amazing playground, and on other days it's like a dilapidated room where you can't find anything.

This book included interviews with people going through different transition processes, including athletic, military and civilian transitions. However, the primary purpose and focus of this book was to examine athletic transition. A great deal of emphasis must be placed on beginning the planning for the post-retirement career you want, as soon as you get into your professional athletic career.

The journey into athletic retirement revealed that athletes go through a mixture of positive and negative experiences during their transition. Some of the negative experiences they faced according to researchers and this work include loss of identity, lack of clarity on new goals, unable to figure out the next mission, struggle to move forward as a non-athlete, loss or lack of purpose, loneliness, disconnection, depression, increased risk of addiction, financial issues, changes in relationships, reduced wellness and health, and increased fears of the unknown.

What we see is that retirement had both positive and negative aspects for all three groups examined—military retirement, civilian retirement and athletic retirement. What seems to be key for all of them is how each person prepared for his journey in retirement, and what skills and resources he was able to bring to bear.

Overall, what we found is that athletes go through several stages when it comes to transition including ambivalence, a searching phase, an anxiety phase, and an epiphany stage. This is true for non-athletes and athletes. Many athletes, as well as non-athletes, we spoke to talked about how nice it was to have the freedom from the rigor of work.

The road ahead is yours to chart. The ups and the downs are yours to face. But this retirement journey can be made easier with the help of others. You are stronger than you think. With hard work and intense introspection you will make it to the other side of your retirement. Be honest with your process and embrace the journey.

## Coping Strategies to Handle Transition

1. Find a passion outside your career. Something that will make you want to get up in the morning.

2. Take the free Myers-Briggs test online (link in Resources section).

3. Save your money. Money gives you the time to transition properly.

4. Go back to school to finish an undergraduate degree or get a graduate degree.

5. Find a sport hobby that will be fun for you: lots of people play golf.

6. Read books on transition and/or visit websites solely focused on changing course (https://changingcourse.com/).

7. Join an association for retired athletes, or other retired professionals.

8. Have (and keep) friends who love you as a regular person rather than an athlete.

9. Set realistic timeframes and expectations. Nothing happens overnight so approach your transition with a positive, patient, and proactive attitude and you will be able to endure the bad days and enjoy the good ones.

10. Celebrate the new chapter in your new life after a short time of grieving the loss of your sports career. Acknowledging that a door is closed is psychologically healthy; spending your time staring at it is not.

11. Enroll in community classes and workshops, including some fun ones like art, dance, drama, or writing. Technical colleges often offer free business courses.

12. Attend and join Chamber, Rotary, Kiwanis, and Elk meetings to see where you best fit, and to make networking contacts.

13. Reach out to your role models to talk through your anxiety, ask questions, and develop a plan of action.

14. Use a free online design program like Canva.com to create a personal infographic (include a short bio, highlights of your strengths, and how you have helped others).

15. Make yourself useful to your community. Team up with recovery and/or transition houses and offer to give power talks about overcoming adversity and your transition journey. In giving, you will build yourself up.

16. Volunteer in a soup kitchen or food bank.

17. Help build a home for someone in need with Habitat for Humanity.

18. Leverage your job title as a retired pro athlete to connect with corporation heads.

19. Consider alternatives to a "regular" j-o-b. Self-employment requires a boatload of self-discipline but also offers freedom of time and schedule. It's not necessarily about what you're good at, it's more about what you LOVE to do.

20. Take a vocational course that interests you on a test drive with *pivotplanet.com*.

21. Start a Business: Business innovation can play a role in creating opportunities for retired athletes. For example, on January 11, 2017, hip hop musician and actor Ice Cube and entertainment executive Jeff Kwatinetz started the Big3 basketball league for retired NBA and international basketball players. This 3-on-3 half court basketball league operates in 18 venues, and consists of 12 teams, 72 retired Hui players and 12 coaches. As SB Nation's Ricky O'Donnell reported, players in the league received $10,000 per game last season. Assuming that number remains the same, it equates to $90,000 per player in 2019 over the span of nine weeks.

# Acknowledgements

I sincerely thank Ben Brown for helping to contact contributors for this work. Dr. Alison Pope-Rhodius has been involved in this work from the beginning from my thesis that I wrote for my master's in sport psychology to her contribution here. I am thankful to Stephen Eriksen for also helping me contact contributors, but more importantly, being a voice pushing me forward. Chris Navalta has been an invaluable resource for helping me transcribe my thoughts as well as asking me the important questions to draw out my story. Thank you so very much Tommy Texeira for all the table reads and inspiration.

Thank you to Michelle Hill and the Winning Proof team: Michael LaRocca, Michael Scott. Thank you to my publisher, Drew Becker of Realization Press. Much gratitude goes to Jay and Joan Mandle, my adoptive parents, for continuing to bring a red pen and brutal constructive feedback and needed suggestions to my work. Your guidance and love have been an inspiration to me on my life journey.

Finally, I thank all the participants who were involved in this project. Thank you for all your time you shared with me, but above all thank you for your honesty and courage in undertaking this public project. All the contributors who, by putting pen to paper, were able to not only bring their amazing experiences to life but also open a window to their souls, giving us an incredible view. These contributors are included on the following pages.

*Adonal Foyle, MA, MBA*

**Professional Athletes:** Athletic Retirement

Roy Byrd: Former Harlem Globetrotter

Ruthie Bolton: Retired WNBA player

JJ Stokes: Retired NFL Wide Receiver

David Vaughn: Former NBA player

Mark Munoz: Retired Mixed Martial Artist (UFC)

Kristi Yamaguchi: Retired Professional American Figure Skater

Bret Hedican: Retired Professional Hockey Player

Brent Jones: Retired NFL Tight End

Shaun Livingston: Former NBA Player

Marc Jackson: Former NBA Player

Bob Delaney: Retired NBA Referee

Alexus Foyle: Former International Basketball Player

Ana Julaton: Professional Boxer and Mixed Martial Artist

Mark Blount: Former NBA Player

**Military Retirees:** Military Retirement

Roy Byrd, Sr.: Vietnam War Veteran

Ryan-Thomas Brown: Veteran, US Marine Corps

Juan Carlos Gomez: Retired, US Marine Corps

**Civilian Retirees:** Civilian Retirement

Sharon Ann Cohen: Business executive

Norm Sobel: Sales executive

# Resources

**National Basketball Retired Players Assoc.**

Phone: 312-913-9400

*Website: http://www.legendsofbasketball.com/*


**Wounded Warrior Project**

Phone: 877-832-6997 or 904-296-7350

*Website: https://www.woundedwarriorproject.org/*


**U.S. Dept. of Veteran Affairs**

Phone: 844-698-2311

*Website: https://www.va.gov/*


**Social Security Administration**

Phone: 800-772-1213

*Website: https://www.ssa.gov/*


**NBPA (National Basketball Players Assoc.)**

Phone: 212-655-0880

*Website: https://nbpa.com/*

**NBA**

*http://www.nba.com*

**Valerie Young**

*http://www.changingcourse.com*

**National Suicide Prevention Lifeline**

800-273-8255

**Free Online Therapy & Counseling**

*https://www.7cups.com/*

**Free Crisis Text Line**

*https://www.crisistextline.org/*

**HopeNet360 Online Crisis Chat Line**

*https://hopenet360.com/*

1-800-273-TALK (8255)

*Adonal Foyle, MA, MBA*

## *Free Career Assessment Tools:*

**Myers-Briggs Personality Assessment**
*http://www.myersbriggs.org/*

**Keirsey Temperament Sorter**
*https://www.keirsey.com/sorter/register.aspx*

**iSeek Career Clusters**
*https://careerwise.minnstate.edu/careers/clusterSurvey*

**My Next Move Interest Profiler**
*https://www.mynextmove.org/explore/ip*

**Holland Code Career Test**
*https://www.truity.com/test/holland-code-career-test*

**The Scars Foundation:**

Founded by Sully Erna and Godsmack to help raise awareness of the mental health issues that so many are faced with today. Because of the rise of suicides, bullying, addiction, and abuse, the Scars Foundation is dedicated to providing resources and tools to educate and empower people on a global level.
*https://www.scarsfoundation.org*

# About the Author

Adonal Foyle, MA, MBA is a retired NBA player, who was the eighth overall pick in the 1997 NBA draft. He played a total of 13 seasons, the first ten with the Golden State Warriors and last three with the Orlando Magic. Upon his retirement from playing professional basketball, Adonal served for two seasons with the Orlando Magic as their Director of Player Development.

Adonal grew up in the tiny nation of St. Vincent and the Grenadines, where he first picked up a basketball at the age of 15. His quest for a college education that ultimately led him to the United States and into the NBA is an amazing and inspirational story of ambition, hard work, and a little bit of luck. Growing up in impoverished circumstances in the Caribbean dramatically influenced Adonal's worldview, and off the court he has always been an activist with a deep commitment to the community, especially young people.

Despite being recruited by several top basketball colleges, Adonal made the unorthodox decision to attend Colgate University, a small liberal arts college in upstate New York. A major factor in his decision was his desire to leave college with a strong academic grounding. At Colgate, with 492 career blocks, he set an NCAA record, which was broken in 2002. Although he left Colgate early to join the NBA, he maintained his commitment to education and graduated in 1999.

*Adonal Foyle, MA, MBA*

During his NBA playing days, Adonal was a defensive specialist, collecting over 3,400 rebounds and bringing toughness and tenacity to every game. He holds the Warriors' franchise record for blocked shots at 1,140. He was also a member of the 2009 Eastern Conference Champion Orlando Magic.

Adonal has received many honors including induction into the World Sports Humanitarian Hall of Fame and the CoSIDA Academic All-America Hall of Fame, NBA Players Association Community Contribution All-Star Award, Social Change Agent (Greenlining Institute), NBA Community Assist Awards (multiple years) and was named Runner-Up Central Floridian of the Year by the *Orlando Sentinel* in 2010. He has also been appointed as a Goodwill Ambassador for St. Vincent and the Grenadines and has been honored with his own national postage stamp.

A published author, national speaker, and consultant, Adonal resides in Northern California and enjoys reading, wine tasting, racquetball, traveling, and writing poetry.

# Connect with the Author

*www.AdonalFoyle.com*
*www.FoyleConsulting.com*
*Twitter.com/afoyle3131*
*Facebook.com/FoylesForum*
*Linkedin.com/adonalfoyle*

# Other Books by Adonal Foyle, MA, MBA

*Too-Tall Foyle Finds His Game* is the first in the Too-Tall Foyle series. Too-Tall Foyle is having trouble finding a sport that fits his abilities and the other kids keep laughing at him. Will he give up sports entirely or finally find his game? The Too-Tall Foyle series is perfect for children aged 3 to 8 years old. Written by Adonal Foyle & Shiyana Valentine-Williams; illustrated by Toni Pawlowsky (Paperback, 8.5" x 8.5", 24 pages, color).

Available at Foyle31.com or through Amazon

*Too-Tall Foyle Makes the Team* is the second in the Too-Tall Foyle series. Too-Tall's adventures continue when he makes new friends, faces new challenges, and learns new skills on his way to making the team! Written by Adonal Foyle & Shiyana Valentine-Williams; illustrated by Toni Pawlowsky (Hardcover, 24 pages, color).

Available at Foyle31.com or through Amazon

*Too-Tall Foyle's ABC's*
In this third book in the series, Too Tall takes the alphabet on a full-court press of basketball tie-ins and action!

Available at Foyle31.com or through Amazon

*In The Athlete CEO,* Adonal Foyle presents seven matrices: Personal, Professional Sports, Family, Financial, Public, Charity, and Post-Career. The overall takeaway is that he wants athletes to appreciate what they already do on a day-to-day basis. By managing numerous elements of their lives, they are already doing the work of an Athlete CEO.

*Written by Adonal Foyle*

*Paperback, 6" x 9", b/w*

*Available at Foyle31.com or through Amazon*

*When the Ball is Laid to Rest* Capturing over three decades of poetry and prose, *When the Ball is Laid to Rest* takes you on the journey from a small dark island in the Caribbean to the bright lights of Madison Square Garden. Filled with joy, pain, and dreams, *When the Ball is Laid to Rest* is a must for the poetry fan in all of us.

*Available through www.AdonalFoyle.com*
*Also available through Amazon*

## Adonal Foyle, MA, MBA

*Drivers of Athletic Success Workbook*

A comprehensive, self-paced workbook that lays out the fundamentals of achieving peak performance.

*Available through www.AdonalFoyle.com*
*Also available through Amazon*

*Drivers of Athletic Success Journal*

A companion book to Drivers of Atheletic Success Workbook to journal about the impoertant concepts in the workbook. The reader can enter his or her thoughts about numerous quotes by athletes.

*Available through www.AdonalFoyle.com*
*Also available through Amazon*

*Winning the Money Game - Lessons Learned from the Financial Fouls of Pro Athletes* offers an abundance of guidance on how to avoid the financial fouls that athletes often find themselves making as they burn through millions of dollars on women, large entourages, family gifts, gambling debts, and even shark tanks. Adonal provides straightforward guidance on a wide range of money matters, from taxes to alimony, from child support to medical bills. He lays out the essential do's and don'ts to help you spend, save, and grow your money wisely. *(Paperback, 8" x 5.4", 193 pages, b/w).*

www.AdonalFoyle.com
ISBN: 978-0-06-234260-7

# ORDERING INFORMATION

For more information and to order copies, visit:

*www.Foyle31.com*

*www.TheAthleteCeo.com*

*www.TooTallFoyle.com*

*www.Amazon.com*

*www.BarnesAndNoble.com*

# References

Jeff Roberts, The Record: "Many Retirees Aren't Prepared for Post-Professional Days," April 19, 2011

Jill Martin Wrenn, CNN.com: "The End Game: How a Sports Star Battled Through Retirement," January 7, 2013

Marty Smith, ESPN: "How Do You Cope When It's Over?" May 10, 2012

Emma Vickers, Sports Psychology: Life After Sports: Depression and Retired Athletes, October 14, 2013

David Wallis, The New York Times: Help for Pro Athletes When the Cheers Stop, May 9, 2012

Dr. Riley Williams III, HSS.edu: "What Do Pro Athletes Face After Retirement? May 24, 2013

Ian Sager, Bloomberg Businessweek: "Life After Sports," January 4, 2007

Thomas L. Schwenk, Daniel W. Gorenflo, Richard R. Dopp and Eric Hipple: "Medicine and Sciences in Sports & Exercises" Basic Sciences — Epidemiology," Depression and Pain in Retired Professional Football Players, 2007

Tim Reynolds, Associated Press "Chris Bosh talks about getting a 'taste of retirement'. January 5, 2017

Ali Thanawalla, NBCSports.com: "Lincecum Reveals He Hasn't Retired, Is 'Trying to Transition.'" September 29, 2019

ESPN.com "Transcript of Peyton Manning's Retirement Speech." March 7, 2016.

Sara McNamara, Military.com: "The Top 5 Challenges Veterans Face Today," November 21, 2019

Kendra Chery, BillyPenn.com: "Moses Malone, Darryl Dawkins and the Scary Trend That's Killing so Many Legendary NBA Bigs," October 10, 2015

Kelli Tennant: "The Transition: Every Athlete's Guide to Life After Sports," April 23, 2019

Chris Dudley: "Money Lessons Learned from Pro Athletes' Financial Fouls," May 14, 2018

Rohan Nadkarni: "Dwyane Wade Opens Up About Life After Basketball," February 19, 2020

Garrett Parker, MoneyInc.com: "20 Retired Pro Athletes Who Now Work Normal Jobs," May 3, 2016

www.ingramcontent.com/pod-product-compliance
Lightning Source LLC
Chambersburg PA
CBHW072005110526
44592CB00012B/1212